# CHARTER

## BY

## Renee Ellis

Copyright © 2023 Renee Ellis

All rights reserved.

No portion of this book may be reproduced in any form without written permission from the publisher or author except as permitted by U.S. copyright law.

# "FOR MY SON"

# TABLE OF CONTENTS

Table Of Contents ................................................................. 4

Summary ................................................................................. 1

Intro ........................................................................................ 2

Chapter 1 What is a Public Charter School ....................... 5

Chapter 2 Too good to be true? ......................................... 13

Chapter 3 Getting In ............................................................ 16

Chapter 4 Diversity ............................................................. 19

Chapter 5 Who am I? .......................................................... 25

Chapter 6 Neurodiversity ................................................... 32

Chapter 7 Words I Never Thought I'd Hear….................. 53

Chapter 8: Cruel & Unusual ............................................... 72

Chapter 9 IEP/504 ................................................................ 95

Chapter 10: 504 .................................................................... 98

Chapter 11 IEP ................................................................... 107

Chapter 12 FBA ................................................................. 116

Chapter 13 BIP .................................................................. 121

Chapter 14 OCR ............................................. 123

Chapter 15 A Break ....................................... 132

Chapter 16 NCDPI ........................................ 135

Chapter 17 The Process ................................. 138

Chapter 18 Our 1st DPI Experience ................ 141

Chapter 19 Child Find ................................... 146

Chapter 20 Our 2nd DPI Complaint ................ 149

Chapter 21 The Others… ............................... 160

Chapter 22 What are the kids saying? ............ 171

Chapter 23 Media .......................................... 174

Chapter 24 FIOA ........................................... 183

Chapter 25 Truitt's Parents Advisory Commission ........ 194

Chapter 26 What does change look like… ...... 198

Conclusion .................................................... 204

Epilogue ........................................................ 208

# SUMMARY

When an 8-year-old autistic child expressed a desire to end their life due to feelings of inadequacy, it shed light on the deep flaws within the education system. The child's mother, who had already faced punishment from the school for advocating for her child, intensified her efforts. She embarked on a mission to hold the school accountable, using their misconduct as a glaring example. Her goal was to ensure that children with disabilities are treated with the respect and care they deserve. Recognizing the importance of educating parents about their rights, she dedicated herself to providing a step-by-step guide through these complex processes. By engaging with parents and students, she expanded her knowledge to better assist others in understanding their rights.

While this story may be difficult to digest, it offers validation through empathy. Knowing that others have faced similar challenges often empowers individuals to take a stand. This narrative, rooted in truth, provides a roadmap for those ready to advocate for change. The school not only failed the child in question but also neglected him and then attempted to cover up their actions.

# INTRO

The rollercoaster of emotions I have experienced throughout this past year has often left me deeply concerned. The anger that has pulsed through my veins during this process has, at times, frightened me, triggering a fierce protective instinct akin to that of a mother bear. There were moments when I questioned if pursuing an assault charge would be worthwhile. It seemed as though the system had no shortage of criminal defense attorneys but finding one willing to take on a case involving wrongdoing against a child proved nearly impossible. It might have been more affordable to take that route, but would it truly make me feel better? I have a child who watches my every move. I begged God for the strength to navigate this situation with tact and grace.

Frequent disagreements with my husband became a common occurrence, as his reactions often diverged from mine. He processes upsets differently than I do, and on most days, I consider that a blessing. The countless hours spent writing to every news and media outlet in the area, pleading with them to listen to our story, only to discover that the school might have been silencing them through their "media relations," has been disheartening.

I can't fully convey the depths of hopelessness, and it's incredibly challenging to describe the struggle of not succumbing to their belief that I was in the wrong. I am not irrational; I am a mother fiercely battling a school backed by wealth rather than integrity.

It wasn't until I finally mustered the courage to share my story that I realized I wasn't alone. Other parents, driven by desperation, began reaching out to me for support. Through this journey, I've gained invaluable insights and will continue to educate myself about what equal educational opportunities truly entail. I must confess though, that I lost sight of the ultimate objective more than once during this ordeal. Our goal is to eradicate this issue and impart knowledge to others through our experiences.

Many parents deal with the harsh realities of employment and limited resources. I work full-time, and I am not as restrained by limited resources as many; I am fueled by determination and tenacity. Often, my persistence is propelled by sheer spite. Thus, as countless other despairing parents scour the internet and social media groups for answers, I felt compelled to persevere.

My son no longer attends that school. Yet, as I've mentioned before, the solution isn't to withdraw students from all of these schools; it's to stand up and demand accountability from educational institutions.

When I asked my son if he was okay with me sharing his story to help other kids, he didn't hesitate and said, 'YES. If it helps other kids not feel sad like I did, yes.' I am incredibly proud of that boy, and I can't fathom how someone in the field of education could prioritize anything other than these remarkable children.

I also want to clarify my intentions before delving into this story in case they get lost in the wording. My experience at a North Carolina charter school does not imply that every school operates this way. The spectrum of their practices ranges from the good to the bad and, unfortunately, to the downright evil. I want to emphasize that this story is not a blanket for all charter schools. There were exceptional teachers at our charter school, and the institution itself has the potential to be outstanding. This narrative serves as a guide, aiming to merge personal experience with helpful, practical solutions.

I did my best to navigate through the existing system, and at times, I found some success. However, the process was unfamiliar to me. I invested thousands of dollars in attorneys hoping they could guide me onto the next steps. I asked questions, putting my trust in the established procedures. I realized that understanding these processes in depth could significantly improve the outcomes. Often, I felt like I was in a vast room surrounded by people who were betting on my failure, unsure of which door to open next.

I firmly believe that education equates to power, extending beyond mere basic knowledge. Personally, I learn best when I can relate to the material. My hope is that while readers may not directly relate to my exact story, they will remember that there is no scale to measure the levels of wrong and really wrong; they are one and the same. I often think of Ida Tarbell, a woman of her time, who wrote with intention and the desire to inform.

The notion that I could challenge a system just by speaking out thrilled me; it is in my nature to embrace challenges. As Mother Teresa wisely said, 'I alone cannot change the world, but I can cast a stone across the waters to create many ripples.'

# CHAPTER 1
# WHAT IS A PUBLIC CHARTER SCHOOL

What is a public charter school? A public charter school is a type of school that operates independently but is still funded by taxpayer dollars. Unlike traditional public schools, charter schools have more freedom and flexibility in their educational approach, curriculum, and management. They are publicly funded and tuition-free, which means they do not charge students for attending.

One of the key features of charter schools is their exemption from many of the rules and regulations that apply to traditional public schools. This flexibility allows charter schools to experiment with innovative teaching methods, specialized curricula, and unique approaches to education. Charter schools are often established to provide parents and students with alternative educational options that may better meet their needs and preferences.

In North Carolina, charter schools receive funding primarily from state and local tax dollars. The funding they receive is determined based on a predetermined allocation per student, as set by the local education agency (LEA). This funding model means that charter schools receive funding based on the number of students enrolled, similar to how traditional public schools receive funding.

Charter schools are accountable for their performance and are typically overseen by an authorizing body, such as a local school district or a state education agency. This oversight helps ensure that charter schools maintain high academic standards and provide quality education to their students.

Public charter schools play a crucial role in our education system by offering parents and students an alternative choice, fostering diversity, and encouraging innovation within the educational landscape. In states like North Carolina, the process of establishing a charter school is surprisingly accessible. All it takes is a dedicated group of individuals willing to come together and form a board. This board holds the key to shaping the future of the school.

The process begins with the board developing a comprehensive plan that outlines their educational vision, curriculum, and goals. Once this plan is meticulously crafted, it is presented to the North Carolina Board of Charters for approval. This step is vital, ensuring that the proposed school meets the necessary standards and regulations set forth by the state education authorities.

Upon gaining approval, the board shoulders the responsibility of constructing the school building and covering the associated costs. This financial challenge is often met through various means, with one common method being the issuance of bonds from capital investors. These bonds serve as a lifeline, providing the much-needed funds required to build a conducive and inspiring learning environment for the students.

What makes the journey of establishing a charter school even more intriguing is the diverse range of investors who show interest in supporting these institutions. In some cases, charter schools manage to secure substantial funding from out-of-state investors, showcasing the widespread appeal of these educational models. For instance, in our case, we discovered that multi-million-dollar bonds originated from investors residing outside North Carolina. This influx of capital from external sources not only highlights the appeal of charter schools but also emphasizes the confidence that investors have in the innovative and diverse educational approaches offered by these institutions.

This external financial support underlines the broader impact and recognition of charter schools beyond regional boundaries. It signifies the growing awareness of the importance of empowering local communities through education, fostering a sense of collaboration and shared responsibility in shaping the future of our nation's youth.

In essence, the ability of charter schools to attract funding from a diverse range of investors reflects the flexibility and entrepreneurial spirit inherent in these institutions. By providing an alternative choice in the public education system, charter schools empower parents and students while contributing significantly to the overall evolution and enrichment of the educational landscape. They pave the way for a brighter and more innovative future for generations to come.

The situation at hand raises fundamental questions about the town's procedures for approving out-of-state bonds, especially considering that these bonds require the mayor's endorsement. This intricate process sheds light on a broader issue: the use of out-of-state funds for state-funded schools, a topic that has sparked heated debates within the community.

Delving deeper into this matter, it becomes evident that utilizing funds from external sources for local educational institutions is a contentious issue among the town's residents. One group adamantly opposes this practice due to a valid concern: these out-of-state investors anticipate repayment, often with substantial interest. This repayment obligation can divert a significant portion of the state tax dollars that were originally earmarked for in-state education. Consequently, instead of bolstering the local education system, these funds might inadvertently end up stimulating another state's economy.

This dilemma not only underscores the financial intricacies of education funding but also raises ethical questions about the priorities of the town's leadership. Should the focus be on nurturing the local educational infrastructure, ensuring that the state tax dollars directly contribute to the growth and development of in-state schools? Or is it more beneficial, from an economic standpoint, to seek external investments, albeit at the risk of diverting funds away from the local community?

Furthermore, this situation prompts a critical examination of the town's policies and regulations governing financial decisions. Are there adequate safeguards in place to prevent potential economic leakage, wherein money that could have revitalized the town's own educational institutions instead bolsters the economy of another state? Perhaps there is a need for a comprehensive review of the approval process for out-of-state bonds, aiming for a balanced approach that takes into account both economic considerations and the welfare of the local community.

The issue of using out-of-state funds for state-funded schools transcends a mere financial debate; it delves into the heart of the town's identity and priorities. As the community grapples with these complex questions, a thoughtful and inclusive dialogue among its members, policymakers, and educational experts becomes crucial to finding a resolution that aligns with the collective vision for the town's future.

After finalizing the construction details and preparing the physical infrastructure, the school has the freedom to craft its own unique curriculum and academic calendar, tailored to meet the diverse needs of its students. Though in many cases the words tailored, and diversity don't typically go together, at least that was my experience.

North Carolina, charter schools enjoy unparalleled flexibility in shaping their faculty. Unlike traditional schools, charter schools in the state have the liberty to hire nonlicensed teachers. The state only requires 50% of their teaching staff to hold teaching licenses. This freedom fosters an environment of innovation and diversity, where educators bring a rich tapestry of experiences and expertise into the classrooms.

Moreover, charter schools in North Carolina are not bound by rigid classroom ratios, granting them the flexibility to optimize their learning spaces according to the specific requirements of their students and the demands of their curriculum. This adaptability paves the way for dynamic and engaging learning environments, where teachers can tailor their instructional methods to individual student needs, ensuring a personalized and enriching educational experience for every learner. Again, this was not the case in our experience, our charter school actually had larger classroom sizes, compared to the surrounding public schools.

Charter schools operate independently of elected officials, which means they have a certain degree of autonomy that traditional public schools do not have. This independence allows them to make decisions regarding their curriculum, teaching methods, and overall approach to education without direct intervention from local government bodies. However, this freedom from oversight has begun to raise concerns.

One significant aspect of charter schools' independence is their freedom from the need to address the concerns of parents and taxpayers in the same way traditional public schools do. While public schools often have to answer school boards and elected officials who represent the interests of the community, charter schools have more flexibility in decision-making. This can lead to a lack of transparency and accountability, which is a point of contention in the ongoing debate about the effectiveness of charter schools. The schools become self-governing, and there really is no roadmap to navigate through it.

Another aspect worth noting is that charter schools are exempt from providing transportation services. Unlike public schools that often operate school buses to ensure students can attend classes, charter schools typically do not have the same obligation. This lack of transportation support can create challenges for families, particularly those who do not have access to private transportation or live far away from the school. Our charter school would come to utilize this in negative ways, almost an obstacle designed to remove students from outside the tight-knit confines of this community.

Additionally, charter schools have the flexibility to offer reduced lunches for students in need or even establish their own policies regarding meal programs. While many charter schools strive to provide support for students from low-income families, the absence of standardized regulations in this area can result in disparities between schools, leading to unequal access to essential resources like nutritious meals. Just because a charter school has the ability to implement programs that would otherwise aid in the support of a diverse student body, many don't.

Furthermore, charter schools are not always bound by the same bidding laws that govern public schools. This means they may have more freedom in selecting vendors, contractors, and service providers without necessarily following the competitive bidding processes that public schools are required to adhere to. While this flexibility can sometimes lead to cost-effective solutions, it can also raise concerns about the fairness and transparency of financial transactions within the charter school system. Situations such as the superintendent or the principal having personal gain in the contractor hired to complete a job, are not uncommon within charter schools.

In summary, the exemptions granted to charter schools, including their independence from elected officials, lack of transportation services, varied approaches to providing meals, and freedom from certain bidding laws, are essential elements of the charter school system. While these exemptions provide flexibility and innovation opportunities, they also give rise to important questions about accountability, transparency, and equal access to resources within the education system. As the debate surrounding charter schools continues, finding a balance between autonomy and accountability remains a crucial challenge in ensuring the quality and fairness of education for all students.

# CHAPTER 2
# TOO GOOD TO BE TRUE?

In addition to their flexibility in curriculum design and teaching methods, charter schools offer innovative learning environments that foster creativity and critical thinking. These schools often embrace project-based learning, experiential education, and interdisciplinary approaches, providing students with opportunities to explore subjects in depth and make meaningful connections between different fields of study. By encouraging hands-on learning experiences and collaborative projects, charter schools empower students to develop essential skills such as problem-solving, teamwork, and effective communication. It has been proven that the road to hell is paved with good intentions.

Moreover, charter schools play a significant role in addressing the diverse needs of students. They are able to adopt tailored approaches to education, accommodating various learning styles, abilities, and interests. Charter schools can implement specialized programs for students with specific learning disabilities, gifted and talented programs, or language immersion initiatives. This diversity in educational offerings ensures that students receive personalized attention and support, helping them thrive academically and socially.

Charter schools also foster a strong sense of community and parental involvement. With their smaller class sizes and close-knit environments, these schools often facilitate meaningful connections between teachers, students, and parents. Parents are encouraged to actively participate in heir child's education, collaborating with educators to create a supportive learning environment. This partnership between parents and teachers contributes to a positive school culture and enhances the overall educational experience for students.

Additionally, charter schools promote healthy competition and innovation within the education system. By introducing alternative approaches to learning, they encourage traditional public schools to adapt and improve their methods, ultimately raising the overall quality of education. The presence of charter schools encourages a continuous cycle of innovation and improvement, benefiting students across both charter and public school sectors.

While charter schools have made significant strides in enhancing educational opportunities, it is crucial to address challenges such as equitable funding, accountability, and ensuring access for all students. By addressing these issues, policymakers and educators can work together to maximize the positive impact of charter schools and create a diverse and inclusive educational landscape for students, paving the way for a brighter future.

Furthermore, charter schools provide parents and students with a broader range of educational choices. Families can select a charter school that aligns with their child's specific learning style, interests, or aptitudes. For instance, there are charter schools focused on science, technology, engineering, and mathematics (STEM) education, arts and humanities, language immersion, or vocational training. This variety allows parents to actively participate in shaping their child's educational journey and ensures that students receive an education that suits their individual needs and aspirations.

So, how can this system exist? Charter schools are typically funded by public money, just like traditional public schools. However, they operate independently, often under the oversight of a chartering authority such as a local school district or state education agency. Theoretically, charter schools can provide unique learning opportunities, especially for students at risk of academic failure or those who are academically gifted.

Charter schools receive funding from the state, which means they are obligated to participate in North Carolina's accountability program. They are required to administer end-of-grade and end-of-course tests, ensuring that every student meets the expected standards. I can specifically speak about the dedication to meeting these requirements at the school we attended, and it seems that the commitment to preparing students for state testing is widespread across most charter schools.

In the 2022-23 school year, North Carolina had 206 charter schools serving 138,352 students. Currently, 8.9 percent of North Carolina's 1.55 million school-age children attend charter schools. In the state's public education budget of $11.1 billion, $985 million has been allocated to fund North Carolina charter schools.

# CHAPTER 3
# GETTING IN

North Carolina allows families the freedom to choose their charter school through what is commonly known as the 'Lotto.' These schools are often marketed with the promise of smaller class sizes. However, in our case, when we compared our charter school to the public schools in the area, we found that the class sizes were actually higher at the charter school, accommodating 25 students compared to 18 in the public school. Despite this, the perceived benefits are so attractive to parents that the waitlist for these charter schools stretches into the thousands.

The 'Lotto' system is designed to be blind, meaning that the drawing is conducted randomly. Parents who have completed the necessary admissions requests and documentation could be selected, giving their children the opportunity to attend these prestigious educational institutions. The key aspect of this process is its randomness, although some schools may prioritize siblings or returning students. There's an ongoing debate about what schools are allowed to preselect. The truth remains elusive, and despite the raised questions, the state of North Carolina has established guidelines to ensure equal admission opportunities.

In my pursuit of knowledge, I discovered that in North Carolina, new grants are being offered to promote diversity in charter schools. To be eligible for these funds, charter schools must reserve seats for disadvantaged students. Surprisingly, less than 40% of North Carolina's charter schools have qualified for these grants, and unfortunately, the reasons behind this are evident, which we'll discuss later.

Upon reflecting on our school's admission process, I realized how questionable it was after the fact. Often, it's only in hindsight that we recognize our mistakes. I strongly urge parents to scrutinize the schools they are applying to. Delve deep into the details because this information is frequently not readily available, and you deserve a clear understanding of what you are getting into.

I came across this section from the handbook at my son's former charter school. When this was presented to the Department of Civil Rights, the attorney asked me if I misread this. This excerpt is their policy on admission as it pertains to students with special needs. Not very equal, is it?

Parents of Exceptional Children should provide all student records, along with the latest IEP documentation, to the school's Director of Student Services during the registration process so that the school can ensure that resources and accommodations are in place once school begins. Special services will be rendered to those students who hold prior exceptional certification from another school or qualify for a 504 Plan or IEP. Parents should contact the school's counselor with questions regarding a student's performance or special needs assessment. – Directly from the Charter Schools student handbook

In theory, I fully support these schools 100%. However, having moved from out of state, my experience did not match my initial expectations when I signed up. In my opinion, these schools should be held to a higher standard, considering their designation as 'excellent.' Instead, more legislation is passed, excusing them from accountability. My advice, recognizing that these schools often come with additional support and resources, is to be aware of your rights and understand what they are allowed to do and not do. Don't shy away from asking tough questions and investigating who is actually running these schools; the information is available; you just have to be willing to seek it out.

Moreover, when considering charter schools, parents should thoroughly research policies beyond admissions. This includes examining disciplinary procedures, academic standards, and teacher qualifications, as well as assessing financial stability and turnover rates. Seeking input from current and former parents provides valuable insights into strengths and weaknesses, aiding informed decisions. Additionally, consider the long-term implications, including preparation for higher education or future careers. Carefully evaluating these factors ensures alignment with the child's educational needs and aspirations.

# CHAPTER 4
## DIVERSITY

As I mentioned, my family and I reside in North Carolina and attended a public charter school in the Lake Norman area. This area is named after the large lake located north of Charlotte. This area encompasses several neighboring towns, including Cornelius, Huntersville, Davidson, Denver, and Mooresville. According to the US Census Bureau, Huntersville's population was 63,065 as of July 2022.

Huntersville itself is limited in racial diversity, with 76% of the population being white, 12% black and African American, and a Hispanic population of only 7%. The average household income in this town was $102,000 in 2021.

The charter school we attended also has its own unique demographics. According to US News, there are 500 students enrolled in elementary school alone. The school operates within its own district, a common structure for many charter schools, but it is still affiliated with the larger Charlotte Mecklenburg School District (CMS). This school, featured in my story, has multiple campuses and offers education from kindergarten to 12th grade. Like all charter schools, it is governed by a board, has a superintendent/director, and, of course, the familiar office staff found in all schools. Specifically, the demographic makeup of this charter school consists of 50% male and 50% female students, with 63% of the student body being White, 13% Black or African American, and only 6% Hispanic.

It's important to consider the racial diversity in the student body, including those races that have such low enrollment numbers that they can't be accurately quantified into a percentage. Just because they fall into the 'zero percent' category doesn't mean these students don't attend, or does it? In addition to these concerns, parents should also inquire about whether the school provides cultural competency training for staff and faculty. A commitment to ongoing training in cultural awareness and sensitivity can enhance the school's ability to support students from diverse backgrounds effectively. We are aware that North Carolina is offering additional funds; however, not every school is taking advantage of this opportunity. This situation leaves the door wide open for potential discrimination based on race. While the intention to promote diversity is evident among lawmakers, allowing schools to decide whether they want to engage in this effort seems inappropriate, in my opinion.

Students entering the school's lottery to attend come from various locations, not limited to the Lake Norman area. Charlotte, North Carolina, itself had a population of over 897,000 in 2022. The average household income in Charlotte is $68,000. The city's demographic makeup comprises 44% White alone, 35% Black or African American alone, 14% Hispanic, and 6% Asian. Upon reviewing our school's directory, I discovered that students were commuting from central Charlotte and a few other surrounding towns that are not within the Lake Norman Area.

This data is crucial because, as I mentioned earlier, our story aims to inspire others to stand up for what is right. I developed a great friendship with another mom when our children attended this school together, and I discovered she had experienced what can only be described as racism. I felt it necessary to highlight the racial diversity or lack thereof, within this school because their overall lack of inclusivity extends beyond just skin color.

Yes, we are about to enter into an argumentative and opinionated discussion, so if you feel the need to ignore the realities we face, feel free to think and feel whatever you need to. These stories represent real experiences, and I am doing my best to raise awareness, even though I never claimed it would be easy.

Accusations of discrimination based on race are significant, and something I don't take lightly. However, when there are data, facts, and figures that contradict the explanations given for various actions, it becomes difficult to deny. I won't delve into too much detail about her experience to respect her privacy and know that retaliation is all too real at this charter school. It's worth noting that this school has faced legal trouble in the past due to similar race-related incidents. Obstructing a child's future, simply because of skin color is so far beyond wrong, that I wonder if it's even possible to provide any benefit to a child.

Examining the demographics and the racially motivated bullying occurring at this school across all grades, not just in elementary school, it is crucial to discuss this and demand accountability.

This school has shut its doors to opportunities based on race and disabilities, and the systems in place to protect students are overwhelmed. The issue is that this school does not take kindly to those who challenge them, as I discovered firsthand. The principal informed me that in their 15 years of teaching, they had never encountered a parent like me. Naturally, this was not a compliment, yet I chose to perceive it as one. I proceeded to question them about what set me apart. Was it the fact that I advocated for my child, or was it that I challenged them? At that moment, the meeting abruptly ended, and the police were called. I was no longer welcome at my child's school.

My friend and many other parents have to weigh the option of withdrawing their children and placing them in a potentially worse situation. Take a moment to absorb that. Yes, the thought of withdrawing your child is a gamble, hoping it might be better somewhere else, all because of their skin color, should never have to cross their minds.

While I was advocating fiercely, there were parents at the same school simply striving for equal treatment despite their skin color. I couldn't address this issue without acknowledging this harsh reality, as it urgently demands accountability. I also need to hold myself accountable; I was unaware of their experiences and those of many others, and for that, I am sorry. I was so consumed in my own child's struggle that I failed to even consider theirs. This family not only fights for equal rights but also has a child diagnosed with disabilities, and their journey through the IEP process was very similar to ours. Once again, the fear of rampant racism in our schools has compelled them to stay where they are, making them weigh this option. You tell me, how is this situation beneficial for the child? A way to combat this, especially for any parent reading this who is considering sending their children to a charter school, is to discuss the need for the school to consider parental involvement opportunities, such as parent-led initiatives, diversity committees, or cultural events, which can contribute to fostering a welcoming and inclusive school culture.

As I delved into what felt like an endless sea of legislation and statutes, something caught my attention. In the 2017-2018 legislative session, HB 514 was introduced—an Act to Permit Certain Towns to Operate Charter Schools. This legislation specifically applied to four towns within Charlotte and its surrounding area: Huntersville, Cornelius, Matthews, and Mint Hill. Interestingly, this was treated as local law and did not require the governor's signature.

Essentially, the bill allows these suburbs of Charlotte to establish their own charter schools, with access restricted to local residents only. Furthermore, provision 38.8 grants local municipalities the authority to utilize and increase property taxes to fund these schools. Notably, these four municipalities have predominantly white populations and higher household incomes. These schools would follow the same guidelines as other charter schools in the area, enjoying exemptions from various expectations, effectively granting them a level of self-governance.

In April 2020, a lawsuit was filed by the Committee for Civil Rights and several other organizations, including the NAACP, challenging the constitutionality of the HB 514 bill. The argument made was that this bill violates the state's constitutional guarantees of a uniform system of free public education. However, since there has been no activity under the bill yet, the lawsuit has not progressed.

During my exploration and research on these charter schools, I discovered that local commissioners and government officials are serving on the boards of these charter schools. It's hard to believe that their intentions are solely focused on the child's best interests. In situations where bonds and zoning decisions need approval from a mayor, having the town mayor on the board of a public charter school—especially one that is relatively exempt from explanations to taxpayers—seems, in my opinion, to border on unethical.

I feel like I'm delving into some heavy topics here, and that wasn't my intention. As I mentioned earlier, I support the ideology behind charter schools; it's the lack of accountability that I find problematic. Understanding what a charter school is will shed light on why my hands were often tied in various situations, leaving me with my thoughts and a strong desire to raise awareness through this detailed account.

# CHAPTER 5
# WHO AM I?

It's common for us as parents not to want our children to experience the challenges we face. We strive to shield them from the lessons we learned and the mistakes we made. However, at some point, we have to step back and allow them to make their own mistakes, being there to comfort them when they fall. One of the most challenging aspects of being a parent is figuring out how to prepare our kids for an uncertain future, especially in today's world; even next week feels like a mystery these days.

We cling to these core memories, which many professionals refer to as 'trauma.' As adults, we often make jokes about our childhood experiences and how they have shaped who we are today. Our social construct is something not many of us are willing to truly break down and sift through.

I am in my late 30s, and I never graduated high school. I can recall fragments of my early years, all the way back to kindergarten. I remember crying frequently in the 4th grade, claiming not to feel well, and spending most days in the nurse's office. I wasn't physically ill; it was what I would later learn was overwhelming anxiety. I recall being punished by writing sentences for my lack of impulse control and misbehavior at school. My red Friday folder was consistently filled with marks. I had a habit of picking at my cuticles until they bled. I often craved attention, aspiring to be the star of the show, and I was always dressed up; I was one of those 'watch me' kids.

When middle school arrived, I was sent to live with my aunt. I can't quite recall the reason, and maybe I didn't fully understand it, but I believe it was because I was considered 'unmanageable.' Around the age of 11, I was formally diagnosed with ADHD/ADD. The testing process felt never-ending; I remember going to a small office, and my mom dropped me off with lunch. We played soccer during breaks, and I had to sit in a tiny room answering questions ALL day. For years, I thought my diagnosis resulted from forcing a child to endure hours of uninteresting questions and assessments; any child would break under that pressure.

During middle school, the parent-teacher meetings became more frequent. My mother was a single mom, and taking time off work for these meetings was not something she enjoyed. I recall sitting in a circle of desks in middle school, absentmindedly playing with a paperclip. One of the teachers on my team said, 'Just because you're not looking at me, I know you're listening.' That comment, looking back years later, was a game-changer. I often wonder what happened to that lady; I have no idea what her name was.

'What is wrong with you?' and 'Did you take your meds today?' Those were some of the comments that stuck with me. The feeling of shame and embarrassment in front of a classroom full of what I perceived as 'normal' kids was overwhelming. No one knew how hard I tried to feel just "not good enough." I had started on medication, leading to arguments between my parents. My father didn't think I needed them, while my mother was desperate for a solution. Their separation and lack of agreement meant I often found myself caught in the middle.

Somehow, I made it through middle school and entered high school. The sheer size of my high school brought great diversity, with kids from all walks of life and the independence that comes with growing up. I was still on medication, and I still despised it. I felt constantly tired and in a fog. I remember sitting on the stairs during lunch, wanting to eat but lacking the appetite, which only triggered my anxiety. In class, I tried to focus, but nothing seemed to stick, despite the pharmaceutical assistance.

Every day, I would tell myself that today would be the day I would 'change.' I would focus intently on my handwriting as if that could solve everything. I noticed other girls with elegant handwriting and thought that must be the solution. They didn't seem to struggle; they had plenty of friends and people liked them. They didn't spend weekends in Saturday School or evenings arguing with their mom. But as the class progressed, I found myself struggling to keep up. My attempts at 'pretty handwriting' were failing again. I was just trying to scribble down as much as I could, hoping to study it later when I got home.

No matter what I did, I couldn't retain the information in my mind. I discovered that a fellow student was seeking pharmaceutical assistance, and it happened to be the same medication I had but despised. So, I shared. I thought I was doing something nice and right for once. The medication wasn't doing what it was supposed to anyway, and I had something I could be praised for. Soon after, I started smoking pot, lots of pot. It made me less anxious; I wasn't becoming a better student by any means, but I felt better.

After I was caught with the pot, I was sent away again. The state was different, and so were the kids, but the feeling of never 'getting it' persisted. My new home life was also different. I learned what it was like to live without a stigma. I wasn't a bad kid; I was just the new kid. The woman I lived with had heard horror stories, but years later, she told me that I was not at all what she expected based on what she had been told. I got to experience honest communication and the absence of a reputation and lack of trust hanging over my head. It was truly a fresh start.

However, I wasn't excelling in school. I would complete assignments but, for reasons beyond my control, I often failed to turn them in. Then, one day, I was moved back to my old school, for reasons beyond my control; the place where everyone knew me as 'trouble'. The office staff would instantly assume I was up to no good, regardless of my actions. So, my desire to care slowly dissolved.

After years of schooling, only a couple of teachers stand out in my memory, but there's one English teacher I'll never forget. He used to host creative writing clubs, and had a fascination with warlocks and Greek mythology – topics we had no shared interests in. Yet, he was different. He wasn't judgmental; he exuded calmness and acceptance. He challenged my preconceived notions of 'teacher behavior'. Growing up, all teachers seemed the same to me, and it was rare to find one willing to go beyond the basics. I kept failing quizzes despite taking notes, reading the books, and actively listening in class. I genuinely tried, but the question that always haunted me was, 'What is wrong with you?' 'You know this, so why are you failing?'

One day, this English teacher asked me to come in after school to make up a test. Reluctantly, I agreed. I walked into the room, and instead of handing me the test, he read question number one out loud. We had a conversation about the book, and I answered all the questions. I passed the test, imagine that.

Twenty years later, I reached out to him, and to my surprise, he remembered me. He encouraged me to keep fighting and never accept defeat. Words that could not be more inspirational considering the battle I had embarked on.

What this man did didn't cost the district a dime; it didn't deplete the school's limited resources. He tried something different. However, in the end, my parents decided that I had missed too much, and I had to drop out of school. So, I did. I was withdrawn halfway through my senior year and completed my GED about a month after I left the state.

I was never placed on an IEP or a 504, and to be honest, I don't even know if it was an option back then. There was special education, but the students in that class had severe mental and physical disabilities. Students like me got lost and were punished because no one really knew what was wrong with us, let alone how to teach us. Kids like me were labeled as 'problem kids.'

My fear of learning persisted until my 30s when I made the decision to pursue my bachelor's degree. I can't emphasize enough how challenging it was for me to grasp the basics. I had to teach myself methods and trick my brain in order to learn the material.

I am on track to graduate with honors, and soon enough, I will have 'Dr.' in front of my name. For far too long, I carried my trauma with me. I had to open doors that were shut because of my learning disabilities. The conversation about kids struggling with things beyond their control was not a common one; it wasn't frequently considered. Many children were labeled as 'those' kids, myself included. I understand the pain associated with not having control over how your mind works. I had resigned myself to the idea that I would never receive a proper education, and I couldn't help but feel envious of those who did. It came so naturally for them to pursue a higher education. I had wasted years because of a preconceived notion.

Even as an adult, I was told that managing work, raising a son, and going to school would be too much. Using spite to fuel my ambition might not be the healthiest approach, but it has been effective. As long as I don't let my spite turn into resentment, I believe I'll be okay. I've found a level of acceptance that I didn't have growing up.

I won the science fair in the 3rd grade; it was about the rainforest. I placed first in my small town and then, I got to go to the big city for the state finals, where I placed 3rd. Looking back on that day, that moment; standing on a stage in front of hundreds of people with a ribbon in my hand. I had no idea that moment would be one of the last times I would feel like I was "smart" for a long time. It was easily twenty years later when I could say that I was confident in my ability to do something. I spent years learning about my challenges quietly, and then my strengths and passion started to develop. Today I actually have self-worth; it's a shame it took 30 years for me to realize it. I am now more self-aware than I have ever been and speak openly about my challenges.

So, why do I challenge everyone? It's not just confidence; it's passion. Reflecting on our upbringing and considering what we want to shield our kids from, there are certain challenges that come with parenting, and then there are triggers. I refuse to let my son experience the debilitating feeling of not being good enough, as it can profoundly impact one's sense of self-worth and hinder excellence. Observing his struggles, I've noticed factors beyond his control, and it immediately triggers my fear because it seems like he might have it worse than I did. I could never forgive myself if I didn't provide him with the opportunity to feel confident and create a pathway for him to explore.

I am intelligent, and so is he, but often, people don't listen to us because we don't convey our messages in a traditional way. He will miss curfew, have his heart broken, and he will stumble more than once, but I will never let him feel inadequate; I know that feeling too well, and it hurts.

# CHAPTER 6
# NEURODIVERSITY

Neurotypical is a term that has long been used to describe individuals who think and process information in ways that are considered typical within their cultural context. These individuals tend to learn skills and achieve developmental milestones around the same time as their peers, and their experiences often align with what is widely accepted as the norm. However, this term can sometimes carry the assumption that the neurotypical way of thinking and learning is not only correct but also the only way.

In our educational system, the framework is predominantly designed to cater to neurotypical minds. From standardized tests to classroom settings, the educational landscape is tailored to suit the needs of those who fall within the neurotypical spectrum. This prevailing system may inadvertently overlook the diverse ways in which individuals' brains function and how they perceive the world around them. Consequently, it can create challenges for those who think differently, hindering their ability to express themselves and learn effectively.

This is where the term "neurodivergent" comes into play. Neurodivergent individuals, by definition, have differences in mental or neurological functions. These differences can manifest in various ways, leading to alternative and less common methods of communication and learning. It is estimated that approximately 1 in 5 children are neurodivergent, highlighting the prevalence of diverse cognitive styles within our society.

Contrary to the misconception that neurodivergent individuals are incapable of learning, numerous studies have debunked this notion. In fact, research has shown that these "alternative thinkers" often possess higher IQs and unique cognitive abilities. The Centers for Disease Control and Prevention (CDC) has reported alarming statistics, indicating that 1 in 42 males is autistic, a rate significantly higher than that of females. Moreover, there is a concerning trend of misdiagnosis among females, further emphasizing the need for a more nuanced understanding of neurodiversity.

In recent years, there has been a shift in perspective, acknowledging that neurodivergent individuals possess valuable skills and perspectives that can be advantageous in various contexts. The Harvard Business Review, citing insights from "Psychology Today," has even stated that neurodivergent individuals have a competitive advantage. Their diverse ways of thinking can foster innovation, creativity, and problem-solving skills that are essential in today's complex and rapidly changing world.

As we continue to recognize and celebrate neurodiversity, it is crucial to create inclusive environments that embrace and support individuals of all cognitive profiles. By doing so, we can harness the full potential of every individual, fostering a society where differences are not just accepted but celebrated as strengths.

John Elder Robinson's perspective, as a co-chair of the Neurodiversity Working Group and someone diagnosed with Asperger's Syndrome, sheds light on an essential aspect of the neurodiversity movement. Embracing neurodiversity signifies a shift away from viewing neurological differences as disorders that require a cure. Instead, the focus is on creating inclusive environments through accommodations and support. This approach recognizes that neurodivergent individuals have unique strengths, talents, and perspectives that can contribute significantly to society when given the right opportunities and understanding.

As parents, it is crucial to educate ourselves about what neurodivergence entails. Understanding the diverse ways in which neurodivergent individuals may perceive the world, communicate, and learn is fundamental. By gaining this knowledge, parents can advocate effectively for their neurodivergent children, ensuring they receive appropriate support and accommodations in educational settings.

Moreover, parents play a vital role in advocating for changes within the education system. It is essential to demand that educators become knowledgeable about the signs of neurodivergence and are confident in adapting their teaching methods to cater to diverse learning styles. This includes embracing flexible lesson plans, incorporating assistive technologies, and fostering a classroom environment that celebrates differences rather than facilitating conflict or antagonism by setting such students apart from neurotypical students

Additionally, parents can encourage open dialogue and awareness within their communities. By fostering understanding and acceptance among peers, parents contribute to creating a more inclusive social environment for neurodivergent individuals. Community education initiatives, workshops, and support groups can help dispel misconceptions about neurodiversity and promote acceptance and inclusion.

In essence, empowering parents with knowledge and advocating for inclusive education are essential steps in embracing neurodiversity. By working together with educators, communities, and policymakers, society can create a nurturing and supportive environment where neurodivergent individuals can thrive. It is through these collective efforts that we can build a more inclusive world, where everyone is valued for who they are and what they bring to the table, regardless of their neurological differences.

Neurodivergent children, a term that encompasses individuals with diverse neurological conditions such as autism, ADHD, and other developmental differences, often face unique challenges in social interactions and sensory processing. These children may find it difficult to connect with their peers and might miss common social cues that others easily grasp. Due to their distinctive ways of processing information, neurodivergent children tend to display intense interest in specific subjects, leading them to hyperfocus when engaging in activities related to their passions.

Routine plays a vital role in the lives of neurodivergent children. Predictability and consistency provide a sense of stability and security, making it easier for them to navigate their daily experiences. Disruptions to their routine can be profoundly unsettling and may trigger challenging behaviors as they struggle to cope with unexpected changes. Establishing a structured environment and adhering to established routines can help create a supportive atmosphere for these children to thrive.

Sensory processing differences are another hallmark of neurodivergent individuals. Many neurodivergent children have heightened sensitivities to sensory stimuli such as loud noises, bright lights, or certain textures. These sensory inputs can easily overwhelm their nervous system, leading to sensory overload. The reactions to sensory overload vary widely among neurodivergent children. Some may become visibly anxious, expressing their discomfort through restlessness, or acting out behaviorally. Others might internalize the overstimulation, withdrawing, and shutting down as a coping mechanism. These reactions can further cause issues and problems in their day-to-day life and functionality, relationships, education, and career. The increased levels of anxiety and stress that neurodivergent children or individuals experience due to not being accommodated can result in mental illnesses and physical health conditions as well, such as anxiety, depression, and gastrointestinal problems (IBS, IBD).

Understanding and accommodating these sensory sensitivities are crucial in creating inclusive environments for neurodivergent children. Providing them with sensory-friendly spaces, minimizing sensory triggers, and offering appropriate sensory tools can significantly enhance their comfort and well-being. Moreover, fostering empathy and acceptance among peers and educators can facilitate meaningful social connections, promoting a sense of belonging and support for neurodivergent children as they navigate the complexities of the world around them.

In situations where a child displays poor eye contact, it is essential to understand that their version of polite and attentive eye contact might differ from the societal norm. Neurodivergent individuals, in particular, possess a heightened awareness of their surroundings. Despite not making direct eye contact, they are absorbing every detail—the sounds, smells, and energy around them. Their gaze might not meet yours, but rest assured, their mind is actively processing the information being communicated.

Furthermore, some neurodivergent children may exhibit specific sensory sensitivities, especially concerning clothing. Wearing particular fabrics or textures can be a source of distress, leading them to insist on specific clothing choices. These preferences are not mere whims; they are rooted in the child's need for comfort and emotional regulation. Understanding and accommodating these preferences can significantly enhance their well-being.

In the realm of neurodiversity, physical touch can be a potent trigger for emotions, capable of either exacerbating distress or providing much-needed solace. Effective communication becomes paramount in these situations. By openly discussing boundaries and preferences, caregivers and educators can establish a safe environment where the child feels respected and understood.

ADHD, a prevalent neurodevelopmental disorder, often manifests in ways that society may perceive as "misbehavior." Children with ADHD/ADD may appear inattentive, seemingly ignoring instructions, which can be frustrating for those around them. Their short-term memory challenges necessitate repetition and patience from their caregivers and teachers. Repeating instructions multiple times is not a sign of their defiance but rather a characteristic of their condition.

Fatigue can exacerbate these challenges. Paradoxically, tiredness can trigger heightened energy levels in neurodivergent children, leading to erratic behaviors. Recognizing this connection can aid in managing and anticipating these fluctuations, enabling a more supportive approach.

Another common trait in neurodivergent children is the struggle with impulse control and a limited ability to foresee consequences. They might impulsively blurt out thoughts or interrupt conversations, often without understanding the social nuances involved. Patience and gentle guidance can help them navigate these social interactions, fostering their self-confidence and communication skills.

In summary, embracing neurodiversity involves acknowledging and accepting these unique traits and challenges. By fostering understanding, patience, and open communication, we can create inclusive environments where neurodivergent children can thrive, express themselves, and be valued for who they are.

Neurodivergent children, including those diagnosed with conditions like dyslexia and dysgraphia, frequently encounter challenges that hinder their ability to engage confidently in various tasks. These difficulties often manifest when they are required to read aloud, copy information from the board, or comprehend and answer questions related to their reading materials. Despite having the knowledge and skills, these children struggle due to the unique way their brains process information.

In many cases, these children face punishment for their apparent reluctance to complete tasks, when in reality, their brains require alternative approaches to learning. It is crucial to recognize that these challenges are not indicative of a lack of intelligence or willingness to learn. Instead, these children may benefit from accommodating their learning environments to provide them with the support they need.

One effective approach involves creating new pathways for these neurodivergent learners. These new pathways can take the form of accommodations tailored to their specific needs. For instance, providing shorter tasks or breaking down complex assignments into manageable chunks can alleviate the overwhelming feeling these children often experience. Additionally, it is essential to address the emotional aspect of their challenges, such as the fear of humiliation associated with certain tasks.

By fostering a supportive and understanding environment, educators and caregivers can empower neurodivergent children to build confidence in their abilities. Avoiding punitive measures and instead focusing on finding innovative solutions can pave the way for these children to thrive academically and emotionally. Embracing these alternative routes not only benefits the individual child but also promotes inclusivity and acceptance within the educational system, fostering an environment where every child can reach their full potential.

My son was diagnosed with Autism Spectrum Disorder (ASD), General Anxiety Disorder, Attention Deficit Disorder/Attention Deficit Hyperactivity Disorder (ADD/ADHD), Dysgraphia, Dyscalculia, and Sensory

Processing Disorder. In today's understanding and diagnosis, these conditions are often recognized as part of the broader spectrum of autism. Within the spectrum, there exists a wide range of challenges and symptoms, and individuals may also exhibit additional conditions that require specific attention.

The term Autism Spectrum Disorder is comprehensive, encompassing a variety of neurodevelopmental disorders that affect social communication, behavior, and sensory processing. The spectrum is not a one-size-fits-all category; rather, it acknowledges the unique combination of challenges and strengths that each individual may possess. For some, like my son, these challenges extend beyond the traditional boundaries of the spectrum, resulting in additional diagnoses such as General Anxiety Disorder, ADD/ADHD, Dysgraphia, Dyscalculia, and Sensory Processing Disorder.

It's important to note that these conditions are not isolated from one another; they often overlap and interact in complex ways. The field of psychology and psychiatry continues to advance, leading to a deeper understanding of these conditions and their interconnectedness. As a result, healthcare professionals work diligently to provide accurate and personalized diagnoses, enabling individuals and their families to access the appropriate support and resources.

Living with a child who has multiple diagnoses can be challenging, but it's also an opportunity for growth and understanding. By advocating for awareness and acceptance, we can contribute to a more inclusive society that recognizes the diverse strengths and capabilities of individuals on the autism spectrum and those with related conditions. Together, we can create a supportive environment where every individual, regardless of their diagnosis, can thrive and lead a fulfilling life.

Stimming, a term commonly associated with children on the autism spectrum, refers to repetitive or unusual movements and sounds that serve as coping mechanisms and self-soothing techniques. For children with autism, the need to engage in these stimming behaviors can often be indicative of overstimulation. Effective classroom management plays a crucial role in preventing these children from becoming overwhelmed. It is essential to recognize that stimming should not be discouraged or stopped unless it is causing harm, such as in cases of head banging or scratching.

To put it in perspective, consider a more neurotypical example of self-soothing behavior: taking deep breaths in and out when feeling angry. Just like these calming breaths, stimming provides comfort and relief for children with autism, allowing them to navigate a world that can often feel overwhelming.

I, as a parent, have witnessed the challenges my son faces with stimming. There have been instances where he cried out in pain because he couldn't control the repetitive movements, resulting in soreness in his fingers. Over time, we discovered a method that brought him comfort. When he approaches me, I gently hold his hands and rub the tips of his fingers. Remarkably, this tactile interaction soothes him enough to slow down his movements, providing him with the relief he seeks.

It's crucial to recognize that every child is unique; some may crave physical touch, while others might avoid it. Some children may desire hugs only on certain days, while others may seek hugs consistently. The idea that these differences are abnormal is contrary to my understanding. As adults, we often label similar behaviors as preferences. Just as some people enjoy a hot cup of tea to relax, children with autism have their unique ways of finding solace in the world. Embracing these differences and understanding that stimming is a natural response helps create an inclusive and compassionate environment for all children.

Why do we label these children as difficult through their most formative years? Kids will adopt the idea that there is something wrong with them and when they feel they won't be able to do something, there is a good chance they won't even try. It's all relevant, neurotypical is merely a word that need not apply anymore.

Nine times out of ten, neurodivergent children and adults will thrive when the task includes joy for them. If you take one thing away from this entire book, then take this. Neurodivergence is real, and the brain has no control, it's not something that can be punished or even bribed. Often times, the dopamine in the brain acts as a stimulant and can increase focus and lower anxiety levels. Many parents will opt for medication therapy, and that is ok. There is no treatment for these various diagnoses, it's more of a treat-the-symptoms type situation.

Neurodivergent children, those who have neurological differences such as autism, ADHD, or dyslexia, often thrive in environments where relationship-building is emphasized. Establishing personal connections can significantly impact their learning experiences and overall well-being. Fortunately, the Beasly Institute in New Zealand has developed a comprehensive five-step blueprint specifically tailored for designing classrooms and curricula to cater to the neurodivergent mind.

In this groundbreaking blueprint, the institute delves into the intricate nuances of cultivating personal relationships with neurodivergent children. It provides educators with invaluable insights into the benefits of fostering these connections, not just between teachers and students, but also among the students themselves. By understanding and implementing the principles outlined in this program, educators can facilitate social growth among children who may build relationships in ways that differ from the norm.

One of the key aspects highlighted in the blueprint is the emphasis on teacher-student relationships. Educators are encouraged to adopt a patient and understanding approach, recognizing the unique strengths and challenges of each neurodivergent student. By building trust and rapport, teachers create a safe space where neurodivergent children feel supported and valued. This nurturing environment is conducive to learning and personal development.

Additionally, the blueprint addresses the significance of peer relationships within the classroom setting. Neurodivergent children often face social challenges, and fostering connections among students can be transformative. Through carefully designed activities and communication strategies, the program encourages students to interact and collaborate, promoting empathy, understanding, and acceptance. These interactions not only enhance social skills but also contribute to a more inclusive and harmonious classroom atmosphere.

Furthermore, the Beasly Institute's blueprint emphasizes the importance of tailored teaching methods. Recognizing that neurodivergent children have diverse learning styles and preferences, the program advocates for personalized approaches to instruction. By adapting teaching techniques to accommodate individual needs, educators can optimize the learning experience for every student, ensuring that they reach their full potential.

Incorporating these strategies into classrooms not only benefits neurodivergent children but also enriches the educational experience for all students. The cultivation of empathy, tolerance, and acceptance through relationship building fosters a positive learning environment where everyone can thrive academically and socially.

In summary, the Beasly Institute's five-step blueprint serves as a guiding light for educators seeking to create inclusive and supportive environments for neurodivergent children. By understanding the profound impact of personal relationships and implementing tailored teaching methods, educators can empower their students, fostering a sense of belonging and enabling them to excel both inside and outside the classroom.

I make it a point to delve deeply into understanding his diagnosis. I do this not only as a responsibility but also as a labor of love because I am his advocate. In my eyes, being an advocate means more than just offering support; it means becoming a safe haven brimming with unwavering understanding. If I am not the sanctuary where he can freely express himself, where else will he find the courage to be vulnerable and truly let his guard down?

In my journey as his advocate, I have come to realize that assumptions have no place in this role. I never assume that his behavior is intentional. Instead, I firmly believe that his actions are often driven by something else, something that is entirely out of his control. It might be the intricate interplay of emotions, the overwhelming sensations that accompany his diagnosis, or the nuanced challenges he faces on a daily basis.

Empathy and patience have become my guiding lights in this voyage of understanding. Each day, I strive to see the world through his eyes, to comprehend the unique lens of perception that shapes his reality. This endeavor not only enriches my understanding of his struggles but also strengthens the bond between us.

I have learned that being an advocate means being a fierce champion for his rights, a compassionate listener to his unspoken words, and a steadfast pillar of support in the face of adversity. It means advocating for a world where acceptance and inclusion reign supreme, where everyone, regardless of their diagnosis, can navigate life with dignity and grace.

So, I continue on this journey, armed with empathy, knowledge, and an unwavering commitment. Together, we navigate the intricate tapestry of his diagnosis, not just as advocates and individuals, but as partners in the pursuit of a more compassionate and understanding world.

The other thing you must remember is that there is nothing inherently wrong with these kids. They are not inherently flawed or damaged. What often happens is that society imposes certain expectations on individuals, especially young people, shaping their behavior and attitudes. However, if you delve into the pages of history, you'll quickly realize that social norms are not always a reliable measure of what is right or just.

Throughout history, societies have grappled with their own set of norms and values, which have evolved and transformed over time. What might have been considered acceptable or moral in one era might be deemed completely unacceptable in another. It is through social progression, critical thinking, and open-mindedness that we challenge these norms and pave the way for a more inclusive and understanding society.

Social progression is not about discarding traditions or disregarding the values of the past. It's about critically examining these norms, understanding their origins, and assessing their relevance in the context of our rapidly changing world. It is through this process that we develop advancements in various fields, including education, technology, and human rights, that will allow us to reach new levels of compassion, acceptance, and equality.

When we acknowledge that societal expectations can be flawed and restrictive, we empower ourselves to question these norms, fostering an environment where individuals are free to express their true selves without fear of judgment or prejudice. Embracing diversity and embracing the unique qualities of every individual can lead to a more harmonious coexistence, where differences are celebrated rather than condemned.

It is our collective responsibility to challenge outdated norms and advocate for a society that values acceptance, empathy, and equality. By doing so, we can create a world where every individual, including these kids, can flourish and contribute their unique talents and perspectives to the greater good of humanity.

Sir Ken Robinson's TED talk on how the education system stifles creativity has resonated with many people around the world. His insightful observations shed light on the importance of nurturing creativity in children, which is often overshadowed by standardized education practices.

It's essential to acknowledge that amidst the challenges within the education system, there are indeed innovative and progressive educators who recognize the need for alternative learning methods. These dedicated professionals understand that every child is unique, with different learning styles and abilities. They strive to create inclusive environments that cater to neurodivergent students, fostering an atmosphere where creativity and individuality are celebrated rather than suppressed.

In recent years, there has been a growing awareness of the diverse ways in which people learn. Forward-thinking educators are embracing this understanding, implementing teaching strategies that accommodate various learning styles, cognitive differences, and talents. They are encouraging students to explore their passions, think critically, and express themselves creatively.

However, despite these positive efforts, there is still much work to be done on a broader scale. It's crucial for society to recognize the importance of fostering creativity in education and to continue advocating for systemic changes. By supporting and empowering educators who champion alternative learning methods, we can create a more inclusive and nurturing educational environment for all students, allowing their creativity to flourish, and ensuring they reach their full potential.

The school we were at, the one that prompted this book, did not support alternative learning in the slightest. It was ironic, considering the administration repeatedly boasted about their advanced degrees in special education. Despite their impressive credentials, there was a glaring lack of understanding and acceptance of diverse learning styles within the institution. This deficiency not only hindered the growth of students who thrived through alternative methods but also created an environment of frustration and stagnation. This experience served as a catalyst for us to explore the importance of embracing different learning approaches in our educational system. It ignited a passion within us to advocate for inclusive education and inspired the creation of this book, which aims to shed light on the vital need for change in our schools and communities.

I have heard many argue that the classroom disruptions that stem from "those" children impede the learning of the other children. My thought is that if those children don't demonstrate behaviors that could be considered disruptive, it must mean that they are more likely to adapt. Adaptability would mean that if the classroom was managed differently, they would most likely still succeed. If there were fewer behaviors, that would only improve their ability to learn as well.

In the majority of schools, there exists a dedicated department known as the Exceptional Children (EC) department. Within this department, a team of specialized educators takes on the crucial responsibility of ensuring the smooth implementation of accommodations for students enrolled in Individualized Education Programs (IEPs). These accommodations are tailored to meet the diverse needs of students with disabilities, aiming to create an inclusive learning environment.

The EC team plays a multifaceted role within the school system. One of their primary tasks involves meticulously maintaining a wide range of accommodations specified in students' IEPs. This responsibility requires a keen attention to detail and a deep understanding of each student's unique requirements. By doing so, the EC team ensures that every student receives the necessary support to excel academically and participate fully in the educational experience.

In addition to accommodation maintenance, the EC team is also responsible for conducting assessments to gauge student's progress and identify areas where additional support may be needed. These assessments are designed to be fair and comprehensive, considering the individual challenges and strengths of each student. Based on the assessment results, the team implements necessary modifications to the curriculum, teaching methods, or assessment formats to facilitate optimal learning outcomes.

Moreover, the EC team serves as a valuable resource for classroom teachers who may encounter challenges while instructing students with diverse learning needs. Teachers can turn to the EC department for guidance, advice, and collaborative problem-solving. This collaborative approach fosters a supportive educational community where expertise is shared, and students' needs are met effectively.

In essence, the EC department plays a pivotal role in promoting inclusivity, understanding, and success within the school environment. Through their unwavering dedication and expertise, the EC educators contribute significantly to shaping a nurturing and empowering educational landscape for students of all abilities.

In our society, there exists a widespread misconception that neurodivergence is rare and exceptional. However, this perspective only serves to perpetuate the stigma and challenges faced by individuals who fall under this category. By reevaluating our approach and reframing neurodivergence as a natural part of human diversity, we can profoundly impact how we support these individuals, as well as the systems that are meant to assist them.

The burden placed on the department responsible for neurodivergent individuals is immense. These dedicated professionals are tasked with navigating a system that is fundamentally flawed, one that fails to acknowledge the unique needs of neurodivergent individuals. By altering our societal mindset and understanding that neurodivergence is not an exception but a variation within human experience, we can alleviate some of the pressures on this department. This shift in perception allows them to concentrate their efforts on addressing the more complex needs of individuals who require specialized attention and support.

Imagine a world where educators are not only aware of what neurodivergence entails but are also equipped with the knowledge and skills to embrace alternative teaching methods. If teachers were encouraged to recognize the signs of neurodivergence in their students and were empowered to adapt their teaching techniques accordingly, the results could be transformative. Neurodivergent students would no longer be left behind, struggling in a system that doesn't cater to their unique learning styles. Instead, they would thrive, reaching their full potential with the help of educators who understand and appreciate their differences.

Ultimately, the goal of every teacher should be to educate and inspire their students. Embracing neurodivergence as a valuable aspect of our diverse society not only enhances the educational experience for neurodivergent individuals but also enriches the learning environment for everyone. When teachers are encouraged to adopt inclusive practices and celebrate neurodiversity, classrooms become spaces where acceptance, understanding, and growth flourish. By dismantling the notion that neurodivergence is rare and challenging, we pave the way for a more compassionate and enlightened education system—one that truly serves the needs of all students, regardless of their neurological differences.

The current educational system operates in a rigid and linear manner, catering to one way of learning and thinking. However, when these students enter college, they are suddenly expected to engage with complex theories and ideologies, challenging established norms and presenting common knowledge in diverse ways. The goal is to cultivate new perspectives and innovative thinking. Yet, the contradiction lies in the way we restrict students to a single method of learning throughout their earlier education.

In my view, the issue does not lie with the students; rather, it stems from educators who have grown complacent within the confines of this outdated system. To initiate change, we must challenge the very foundation of this educational structure. It's akin to asking students to step out of their comfort zones, something educators and administrators often demand of their students, even if it causes them considerable anxiety, as long as it maintains the comfort of the teachers.

The real challenge lies in convincing the educational establishment that change is not only necessary but vital for the intellectual growth of our future generations. This transformation doesn't have to be a battle, although it likely will be, given the resistance to change that often permeates institutions. My dedication to this cause is fueled by the understanding that there is no magical solution or quick fix. There are no genies in bottles granting wishes; there's only the ongoing struggle and perseverance to demand something better.

By advocating for a more flexible and inclusive educational system, we can empower students to explore various modes of learning and thinking. Encouraging educators to adapt and embrace new teaching methodologies will not only benefit the students but also lead to a more dynamic and innovative society. It is through this collective effort and unwavering determination that we can pave the way for a brighter future, where education truly becomes a tool for fostering creativity, critical thinking, and a thirst for knowledge.

## CHAPTER 7
# WORDS I NEVER THOUGHT I'D HEAR...

On April 25, 2023, a day etched into my memory, my 8-year-old uttered words that shook me to the core. "I feel like I want to hurt myself, I can't do anything right anyway". I asked what he meant, trying to organize my initial reactions, I asked if knew what that meant. He said, "Yes, they want me gone". He confided in me, his voice laden with fear, expressing his overwhelming emotions. In that vulnerable moment, he went on to tell me that the feeling was scary. He had successfully identified the fear attached to suicide; he was 8. The cause of his anguish? His ELA teacher, the very person I had entrusted with nurturing his young mind, became the source of his despair. He had specifically called the teacher out as the reason there was no question.

As we drove home from school that day, we went through the usual routine of discussing the day's events. It had become a daily routine for us, a way to connect and unwind after a day of challenges and triumphs. Sadly, venting his frustrations about this specific teacher had become a regular occurrence, despite my earnest attempts to address the issue. My efforts, no matter how sincere, had proven futile in the decline of self-worth that had consumed my son.

During our conversation that afternoon, we delved into each of his classes, but his focus remained fixated on that one class and the teacher who seemed to be the source of his turmoil. Normally, I would try to find something positive to divert his thoughts, aiming to end the school day on a hopeful note. However, on April 25th, my usual tactics fell flat. He was resolute, refusing to be swayed by any attempt to shift his attention away from the overwhelming negativity he felt.

We pulled into the driveway, and I was honestly at a loss for words. Nothing I said seemed to pull him out of the funk that was consuming him. I put the car into park, unfastened my seatbelt, and turned to look at him. My son sat there, holding his own hands in his lap, his seatbelt still on, and tears welled up in his eyes. I fought back my own tears, my voice quivering, which he immediately picked up on.

I gently said, "Come here," buying myself a few moments to gather my breath. He climbed over the seats, and I moved my seat back so he could fit on my lap. He wrapped his arms around me, and I held him close. I asked him some basic questions to make sure I understood what he was feeling.

I asked him why he wanted to hurt himself. He responded, "I can't do anything right anyway". I told him that was not true… I then went on to tell him how sad mommy and daddy would be if he was not here anymore, or if he was hurt. I could not stop the tears at this point. I went through the entire list of family, friends, and even pets that would be heartbroken without him. I told him about all the things he was capable of, things he had not even begun to fathom.

He said that the teacher would be happy if he did it. I said, "Yeah maybe, but then they win and everyone else loses". That seemed to trigger a slight emotion in him, as the thought processed, he didn't want to let them win. He never wanted to give them any joy, and rightfully so, I felt the same way. I went on to tell him how my life would come to an end if he left this world, and that made him cry harder. This child has so much compassion, and the idea of hurting those he loves breaks his heart. He feels things most 8-year-old boys can't even comprehend. He can sense good and evil and as he has grown up it never ceases to amaze me how he is drawn to some and others, not so much. I have seen this child offer hugs to the homeless without question; his light is contagious and his heart that he wears on his sleeve is huge. I told him that NO teacher should ever make any child feel this bad about themselves. This child has a heart of gold and no one has the right to take such a kind-hearted child away from this world, let alone his teacher.

After what seemed like forever, we started to talk about ways to ignore them, and some coping methods he could use to get through the days. I explained how their incompetence affected their ability to be kind, and that kindness was a requirement to be a teacher… that they were wrong, I tried to drive that point home every chance I could.

I even let him call them by their first name, taking out any respect for this adult. I feel that when you push a child to want to take their own life … that formality is shot to hell. It seemed to make him feel better. I didn't care about how this teacher felt, or what they would think when my son built a wall and a safe headspace to go to, should this feeling arise again.

The problem was my son was not good at disrespect, he never acted out, he was never rude, and he had never had so much as a note sent home for poor behavior. Which meant he would continue to sit there and take this abuse, as he had done all year. That worried me.

I am a firm believer that even adults can be wrong. Simply being an adult does not automatically make someone infallible or always right. It's natural for individuals, regardless of age, to make mistakes or have incorrect beliefs. Growing up I was always told that it was disrespectful to question adults and challenge their reasoning. It's essential to teach children how to question and challenge ideas in a respectful manner. However, the argument that adults are always right is absurd and I simply can't stand behind that idea.

Still sitting in the car on my lap, he started to find his laughter again. We made a plan and we talked about what to do when that feeling came up. I made him stop and look me in the eyes, I said, "You did the right thing". I could not have been more serious about how telling me his feelings was the right thing to do, and I needed him to know that. I told him that I would always be there to help him through whatever it was that he was facing, regardless of who was right or wrong. He would forever have me to help navigate through these feelings.

I must have given him a hundred kisses during the time we spent in that driveway, he was now climbing all over the seats and starting to gather his things. I told him that I was going to reach out to the principal and let them know where he was at with his feelings. I asked him if that was ok, and he said "Yes". He told me that they would not care, I foolishly tried to convince him that he was wrong, that this was a big deal. Little did I know how right he was.

He leaped out of the car and dashed inside. I struggled to breathe; it took immense effort to compose my thoughts, and a feeling of nausea engulfed me. How could I send my child to school, knowing he would be under the influence of this teacher? I was all too familiar with this teacher's behavior, and we had been enduring their problematic conduct throughout the entire year. My interactions with the principal had been similar; I challenged them, posing a threat in their eyes. Now, the only thing that truly matters to me is at risk of being lost due to their actions.

I immediately went upstairs to compose an email addressed to the principal, counselor, and superintendent. In the email, I reiterated what I had just been told and provided a detailed list of examples that had led to these concerns. I requested a meeting as soon as possible to discuss accommodations, specifically asking for placement in an alternative area during the time of this teacher's class.

I was informed that it would take a week before we could meet due to a planned field trip and some other scheduling conflicts. I found it disconcerting that a field trip would take precedence over addressing a child's well-being. Despite my concerns, they declined my suggestions for alternative meeting times, such as before school, after school, or during lunch.

At that time, our son was seeing a therapist regularly who was helping him with communication and organizational techniques to cope with his daily challenges. It was the first time he had faced serious mental health concerns. The therapist expressed a desire to be present at the meeting, but my requests for their involvement were denied by the school multiple times. Frustrated by the delays, the therapist eventually wrote a letter expressing their professional opinion. The principal mentioned that due to my concerns, they couldn't meet sooner. They assured me that the school counselor had met with our son and reported that he seemed happy.

As a parent, I found myself utterly lost and consumed by fear. The one thing that kept me awake at night was the heartbreaking reality that my son came to me, expressing his desire to hurt himself, and my attempts to help seemed futile. Not only did his pain persist, but it also intensified despite my efforts. I couldn't help but wonder, would he ever confide in me again? After school not only shut him down but made things harder for him. Why would he, when nothing seemed to change – in fact, it only seemed to worsen each time he opened up. The haunting thought of coming home one day and finding my child no longer with us torments me almost daily.

I had started to remove him from school the week before the meeting, wanting him to understand that his concerns were being taken seriously. However, after a few days, the teacher began isolating him from his other classes, making him discard his snack during designated times and sit in their class without any valid reason other than asserting dominance.

How do you explain to a child who did the right thing that they still have to endure such mistreatment? How do you swallow this bitter reality, knowing how fragile they are and how thoroughly their spirit has been crushed? The teacher went so far as to withhold rewards, singling him out and making him watch as the rest of the class received prizes, one by one, while he was left empty-handed.

How can a teacher stoop so low? How can any human with a shred of empathy subject a child to such cruelty? And perhaps most troubling of all, how can the school stand by and allow it to happen?

The day of the meeting arrived, and both the teacher and the principal were present in the conference room. However, the counselor and the superintendent, despite our request to have them attend, were notably absent. I was stunned by their arrogance, lack of concern, and overall lack of empathy. I handed the principal the therapist's letter of opinion, but they refused to look at it. I insisted that it was their copy and slid it back in front of them.

The principal asked for examples to understand why our son felt this way. I provided the same reasons I mentioned in the initial email as if our communications leading up to this were lost. My husband and I sat there, dumbfounded, as we were told that our son's suicidal thoughts were merely his "perception" and that he was mistaken. Their way of handling such a serious crisis was absolutely appalling. Not only did they fail to understand the severity of this situation, but they went so far as to completely invalidate his feelings which were supported by valid incidents. Additionally, the school refused to provide any accommodations. If he continued to miss that class, he would fail the 3rd grade, miss field day, and all the enjoyable end-of-the-year activities. He would also be required to make up the time scheduled with that teacher.

I was in shock. My body trembled, and I struggled to contain my anger. I had to muster all my strength not to leap over the table and smack the smug injected-look off her face. Their half-cocked smile reeked of arrogance, making it hard to remain calm. I had to leave the room; the situation was going nowhere.

I stopped by the counselor's office on my way out. As they sat there, staring at me, I said, "You should have been in there." I went on to say, "I don't know how you sleep at night." They just stared at me, and no words were spoken. I walked out of the doors into the front office, where I paced back and forth, trying to decide what to do.

This school clearly did not care about what was in his best interest, or any child for that matter. I told the secretary to call him down; I was going to withdraw him that very second. The secretary tried to console me and assure me that he was safe here. I believed none of it. I can't remember being as torn as I was at that moment. I wanted all the answers, and I wanted to know what the right choice was.

Was I sacrificing his life or was I doing him a favor? I didn't want to add to his trauma, but I also couldn't stand the thought of him enduring more from this school. After much inner struggle, I made the difficult decision not to pull him out. I didn't want to cause him more trauma, but I knew I had to address the situation.

I resolved to talk to him after school, to assure him that this was not over. I promised him that Mommy and Daddy would keep fighting for him and for every other child who felt this way. I vowed to help him find the good moments in his day, encouraging him to focus on those positive experiences and look forward to the exciting end-of-year activities he was anticipating. Despite my own mental anguish, I couldn't let my child be pulled into my personal hell.

My husband and I left the school and promptly reached out to the superintendent. We sent them an email requesting a meeting, despite their lack of response in the initial chain of communications. To our surprise, they wrote back and asked if they could have a phone call with the therapist before our scheduled meeting, and we reluctantly agreed.

It was clear that the school was failing miserably at implementing a crisis intervention plan, which the state of North Carolina requires. The state guidelines clearly state that reasonable accommodations must be made to protect the mental health of the student. The situation underscored the urgent need for the school to address these issues promptly and effectively.

The next meeting was set for another week out. It was during this week that I was banned from campus. This was the 2$^{nd}$ time they ordered me not to come on campus. The first was a "miscommunication" on their part followed by an apology. This one, however, was for allegedly flipping off the principal in the carpool line.

I know you don't know me, however many of those that do can attest that I do things with intention. A secret drive-by flick of a finger is not in my style. I tend to favor the verbiage that accompanies the hand gesture and tend to pair them together simultaneously. So today, on the off chance that they read this book. *FUCK YOU!* I know that was not appropriate or a mature sentence, however, healing happens differently for everyone, and this book has been incredibly healing to write.

The principal went on to explain in their email to the superintendent that the worst part was that I did this in front of my child, implying that was the worst part of this entire fabricated lie. Without hesitation and any explanation from me, the school issued another ban. I was forbidden to go on campus, if I did, I would be arrested.

So, here we are, just two weeks away from school letting out. I find myself unable to step foot on campus for any reason, including drop-off or pick-up, in a school that provides no transportation. My son, struggling deeply, expresses a desire to hurt himself, and it feels like the school couldn't care less. The tumultuous mix of emotions inside me had to remain hidden because I had to stay calm in front of my son. I was not always good at that during this time which only fed my anxiety more that he would not tell me in the future, should he want to take his own life again.

The meeting with the superintendent was moved to a virtual setting, given that I had been banned from campus. As we began the meeting, we were met with the same smirk that we had seen on the principal's face the week before. I began by addressing the ban, as it was a crucial topic for discussion that day. However, the superintendent adamantly refused to lift the ban. I urged them to review the security footage, but they dismissively claimed they had all the information they needed, refusing to consider any proof.

Feeling defeated on that front, I shifted the focus back to our son's well-being. I asked about the school's mental health plan and its procedures for cases like this. Unfortunately, the superintendent evaded the question, refusing to provide any substantial answers. Instead, they turned the conversation back on us, questioning what we had done to support our son's mental health. They probed into his primary care doctor and private healthcare information, leaving us feeling frustrated and unheard.

This meeting was going nowhere, and I felt as though I was in this twilight zone. Was I crazy? Then I remembered there was a term for this type of behavior. "Gaslighting". I had never really witnessed it firsthand, but wow.

We signed off the meeting and just sat there, my husband and I sat in silence. I didn't even know where to start. I made the decision then and there that this was not over. I didn't know what my next steps were going to be, I just knew that this was not over. This was not going to be the end of it, I had refused to accept this as it. Accepting defeat was not an option, not today.

The following week, I had to take my son to his therapist. The school had spoken to the therapist as per their request, although they completely disregarded his professional opinion. As advised by the police department, I reached out to the superintendent, seeking permission to come to the campus. The school was the only entity that could grant me access. I explained the nature of the appointment and stressed how vital it was, given the recent events surrounding my son's mental health.

To my dismay, my request was promptly denied. I didn't give up; I followed up and elaborated on the appointment's importance once more. I emphasized that they were hindering my son's ability to access vital mental healthcare, especially considering his recent suicidal thoughts. Despite my efforts, the answer remained a resolute no.

Every fiber of my being wanted to fight back against their decisions. I was determined not to prove them right; I refused to let their accusations become a reality. I was attempting to demonstrate to my son that doing what is right and speaking the truth would prevail eventually, even in the face of such adversity. I scrambled to get someone to pick him up so I could get him to that appointment.

My nights became consumed with obsessive research, delving into what North Carolina laws allowed in terms of litigation. I also devoted extensive time to understanding harassment charges, preparing myself in case I chose to confront them more aggressively and pursue that assault charge. I reached out to all the major media outlets in the area, but only one chose to pick up the story. Later, I discovered that the superintendent had influential "relationships" that they heavily invested in. It suddenly became clear why the media was hesitant to touch the story; pieces of the puzzle were falling into place.

One night, as I sat in bed, I stumbled across an article that shook me to my core, actually, I came across many articles. The stories centered around "teacher-led bullying." Children had tragically taken their own lives as a direct result of the actions of their teachers. The mere existence of such a topic was deeply unsettling, yet alone so many of them and yet, I found myself irresistibly drawn to delve into each harrowing account. I knew that It was not smart to read them all, especially considering I was already teetering on the edge of sanity due to my intrusive thoughts. Despite my inner turmoil, I continued reading, immersing myself in the pain and despair of these young souls.

As I read through each heartbreaking narrative, I felt a surge of anger and helplessness. These innocent lives had been snuffed out prematurely, and the responsible parties, the very adults entrusted with their well-being and education, seemed impervious to the gravity of their actions.

Fueled by a mix of anguish and determination, I took a bold step. I meticulously compiled all the accounts I had come across and decided to send them to the school principal and the superintendent. In an impassioned email, I detailed the tragic stories, hoping to jolt them into action, into empathy. To my dismay, my efforts were met with a resounding silence. Not a single response came my way, leaving me bewildered and disheartened.

Amidst the heart-wrenching narratives, one story, in particular, etched itself into my memory. It was the account of a ten-year-old fifth-grade boy from Ocala, Florida, who had succumbed to the darkness that enveloped his life. His best friend, grappling with the loss, voiced a sentiment that resonated with me deeply: "He didn't deserve it," he said, "I wish I was there so I could have slapped the gun out of his hand." The struggles this child faced at the hands of his teacher had become a daily ordeal, a relentless onslaught that proved too overwhelming for his tender soul.

The child's stepfather, grappling with the aftermath, reflected, "But I feel like when kids try to go and tell, I think there's a gap in between there because they don't know how to go and speak to adults sometimes." His words struck a chord, highlighting a painful truth – the presumption that adults are always right simply because of their age is a fallacy.

As I read these accounts, tears blurred my vision, and a knot of dread tightened in my chest. This was my deepest fear realized, and tragically, it was not an isolated incident. The stories I had read shattered the common perception of bullying, revealing a darker, more insidious side. The pervasive stigma surrounding bullying typically revolves around children tormenting their peers, but the haunting truth remained largely unspoken – the tormentors could also be the very adults meant to nurture and protect them.

In the face of such profound despair, I found myself grappling with a haunting question: how do you trigger emotion and empathy in someone who appears so profoundly incapable of it? The answer remained elusive, buried beneath layers of societal indifference and institutional apathy. And yet, I clung to a glimmer of hope, a flicker of determination. Perhaps by shedding light on these hidden tragedies, by refusing to turn away from the darkness, we could begin to ignite the spark of empathy in the hearts of those who had grown numb to the suffering of the innocent. Only then, I believed, could we begin to heal the wounds that had been inflicted on these fragile souls, and perhaps, prevent such heart-wrenching tragedies from happening altogether.

Empowered by my newfound determination, I dove into the intricacies of the legal system. Armed with a list of potential attorneys, I meticulously researched and found one willing to hear my story. I recognized that my case was riddled with wrongdoings, but I also understood the importance of organizing my thoughts and stripping away the overwhelming emotions that clouded my judgment. With the guidance of the attorney, I started cataloging the injustices I had witnessed. Together, we meticulously compiled a document, complete with clear bullet points and concise elaborations, systematically laying out the evidence of the systemic issues that plagued the educational institution.

Despite the hefty cost of $350 per hour, I recognized the value of this legal expertise. In those hours, I learned invaluable lessons about the legal avenues available to me. I discovered the intricacies of filing complaints through agencies like the Office for Civil Rights (OCR) and the North Carolina Department of Public Instruction (NCDPI). I familiarized myself with the process of Freedom of Information Act (FOIA) requests, understanding the power of transparency in unearthing hidden truths. The attorney enlightened me about the OCR procedures, providing me with a roadmap for navigating the complex labyrinth of bureaucracy. Each piece of information, each legal avenue, was like a puzzle piece falling into place, granting me a clearer understanding of the battle ahead. That was exactly what it would be a battle, that I would most likely not win.

During our consultations, the attorney not only validated my concerns but also expertly dissected our issues. He categorized our grievances, explaining the nuances between civil rights violations and the subsequent litigation process. Through patient guidance, I began to comprehend the importance of specific keywords and classifications, essential elements that would ensure our complaints were not just heard but thoroughly reviewed. Armed with this newfound knowledge, I felt a surge of confidence and determination. I realized that I was equipped to navigate the complex legal landscape, armed with the tools necessary to fight for justice.

The journey ahead was far from easy. The information I gathered was not readily available, and the process was laden with obstacles. However, I resolved to persevere, not only for my own cause but also for others who might find themselves in a similar heartbreaking situation. I made it my mission to document every step, every hurdle, and every triumph. In doing so, I aimed to create a beacon of knowledge, a guide for those unfortunate souls who would, regrettably, tread the same path in the future.

As I meticulously navigated this intricate web of legal complexities, I knew that my efforts were not in vain. I was not merely seeking justice for myself; I was paving the way for a future where the oppressed could find their voices, and where the silent cries of the vulnerable would be heard. In my pursuit of truth and justice, I had become not just a victim, but a warrior, armed with knowledge and resolve, ready to champion the cause of those who had been wronged.

It wasn't until well after the school year ended that I learned about the 'drafts' the superintendent was requiring from the staff. All communications were supposed to be sent to the superintendent before reaching us. I learned about this through a state FIOA request and received a small batch of documents from the school's attorney. As I meticulously examined each document, I stumbled upon an email I distinctly remembered receiving from the counselor in between our scheduled meetings. In the email, the counselor noted that none of the meetings they had with my son had been 'therapeutic in nature.' This revelation strongly suggested that the principal had been lying.

The copy marked "draft" did not match the one we received. The original unedited document that went to the superintendent from the counselor explained that through their assessment the child demonstrated and expressed depression and engaged in self-harm while in the classroom. The child was banging his head on the whiteboard upset with a mock EOG grade he received.

The copy we received had the words changed from depression to disappointment. I printed both copies out, the draft to the superintendent and the copy we received. I went word for word and was sick when it clicked that the superintendent was changing the words to downplay the severity of the situation.

A licensed psychologist provided an assessment, and it was altered to fit the agenda of the school. This had me livid, and not knowing who I wanted to tell because through all of this, I was learning of deep conspiracy webs that ran way deeper than I could imagine. So, I held on to it – and would later end up filing a complaint with the Civil Rights division for negligence.

As I sit here and reflect on that moment, I find myself recharged to keep fighting. Throughout this process, I have experienced highs and lows, often feeling like I was making no progress. On certain days, my concerns were acknowledged and validated, but on others, they were simply dismissed. I was cautious not to reveal my true feelings and even more selective about whom I shared information with. The level of bureaucracy in the local

Charter school system was astounding; it felt as if I were living in a Reba McEntire song.

I gently reminded my son that I was still fighting for him and that the process required time and patience. I emphasized that reacting impulsively and losing control wouldn't solve anything. I asked him once more if he was comfortable with me sharing his story, assuring him that his privacy would be protected. Without hesitation, he agreed once again.

The one reporter who agreed to speak with us and hear our story went ahead and published the article amid all the chaos, sending shockwaves through our small town. The news spread rapidly, prompting the school to swiftly defend its actions. The reporter conducted himself with utmost professionalism, giving the school an opportunity to present their side of the story, which they did. However, their explanation didn't quite convince the reporter. He called me and expressed his desire to delve deeper into the matter, a proposition I readily accepted. He wanted to speak with the therapist. The school had been asserting that my concerns and requests didn't align with the reality of the situation or with the child's private therapist's perspective.

The reporter took the initiative to contact the therapist and, after their conversation, published an article confirming that the school had disregarded the therapist's advice and highlighting that my requests for accommodations were indeed justified.

Within hours of the story going live, the school sent out an email to all staff, alerting them about the article and reassuring them that there was nothing to worry about. The principal adamantly claimed that the article was entirely false and vowed to get to the bottom of it. However, unraveling their own deception proved to be a daunting task, which ultimately led to inaction on the school's part.

As the initial shock of the article subsided, I chose to let it fade into the background. I was deeply engrossed in the formal complaints and investigation process, and I didn't want to risk jeopardizing any progress. However, what followed the article was undeniably validating. The responses poured in, with individuals sharing their own stories of similar situations. Many could relate, echoing sentiments like, "This was me." Countless people reached out, seeking advice on how to navigate similar challenges they were facing.

I've been contemplating all of this, especially considering the families who lack the financial means to afford legal representation and learn about their rights. I've thought about the mothers of the children who tragically took their own lives, and I can only imagine what they would give to have their children speak up. My child did, and I refused to take that opportunity for granted. I was determined to pull back every curtain and expose the harsh reality of what was truly happening.

# CHAPTER 8:
# CRUEL & UNUSUAL

Experiencing trauma, especially at a young age, can have a profound impact on a person's emotional well-being. When a victim is placed in situations reminiscent of their trauma, it often triggers distressing emotions and memories. In the case of my son, he found himself grappling with the aftermath of multiple incidents that occurred in the 3rd grade, Incidents that left him feeling hopeless.

The catalyst for his trauma was a teacher whose behavior was deeply troubling. This teacher's actions not only shook my son's confidence but also planted the seeds of worthlessness in his young mind. The pain caused by this teacher was so severe that my son contemplated ending his own life, a heart-wrenching testament to the devastating impact that a single person's behavior can have on a child's psyche.

Even after leaving the school, the scars of that traumatic experience continued to haunt my son. In the subsequent years, he exhibited intense reactions towards teachers, driven by a genuine fear that they might resemble the hurtful teacher from his past. The fear was not irrational; it stemmed from a place of genuine vulnerability and a desperate need for self-preservation.

In an attempt to protect himself, my son built himself emotional walls that seemed impenetrable. These barriers, constructed from a profound sense of mistrust, served as a shield against any potential pain. No matter how well-intentioned, and how loving, it was hard for teachers to easily dismantle these walls. My son's self-preservation instincts had kicked in, and his emotional fortress stood tall, making it incredibly challenging for him to trust and feel safe again.

Navigating the aftermath of such trauma requires immense patience, understanding, and support. It is a journey that demands unwavering dedication from both the individual affected and their support system. Together, we embarked on this challenging path, hoping to help my son heal, learn to trust again, and find the strength to dismantle the walls that had been built around his heart and mind.

I too would be lying if I didn't have a chip on my shoulder when it comes to teachers. My issue is assuming that they all have some parts of them that were like the ones we dealt with at our Charter School. I know better, I know that the intentions are not all the same and there are some pretty amazing ones out there, but I still have to talk myself off the ledge. I have to make a conscious effort to give them the benefit of the doubt. This internal rationalization comes easier to me because I am an adult. The ability to rationalize an intrusive thought is not something a nine-year-old should be skilled at, let alone one that surrounds trauma.

The concept of 'cruel and unusual punishment' comes to mind when I reflect on the teacher's wrongdoings. At the beginning of the year, there were high expectations, which is understandable. It's crucial to set high standards for children, often higher than they set for themselves, so they have a goal to strive for. As adults, it's our responsibility to help them realize their potential and guide them along the way.

This teacher was a proponent of 'life lessons.' They frequently referred to enforced independence as an opportunity for a valuable life lesson. While the theory sounds good, the flaw lies in the unrealistic expectation that a third grader should be as independent as the teacher desires. The notion that third graders should mimic adult behavior worries me. While I acknowledge the importance of fostering independence, punishing a child for a lack of it in elementary school is inappropriate.

Our children are being forced to grow up faster than ever before. The exposure to mature content on television alone is enough to rob them of their childhood. It's essential that we strike a balance, encouraging independence while still allowing them to enjoy the innocence of childhood.

My son faced challenges that were beyond his control, much like many other students do every day. The lack of education about neurodiversity and special needs, coupled with a severe lack of empathy, was evident and concerning with this teacher. Additionally, the school's curriculum was predominantly digital. I understand that our society is moving towards a digital future, but I was astonished by how little the teachers actually engaged in traditional teaching methods. In class, they focused on reading novels and working through benchmarks, which is a standard approach.

However, when I was told that my son wasn't listening during reading time, I was a little confused. As it turned out, the teacher had recorded themselves reading the book, uploaded it to YouTube, and made the kids listen to it in class. When I asked my son about it, he explained that sometimes he couldn't hear well and had requested the teacher to increase the volume. I was puzzled – 'volume'? It became clear that the teacher was physically present in the classroom but not really "teaching", at least in the context we're used to. Grading papers did not consume much of their time as the digital approach didn't allow for paper copies. They refused to accommodate my son's 504 plan, which called for paper-based learning.

This might be the way of the world, but my question to the teachers was, how do you connect with your students? It seems that the energy spent creating adults in your $3^{rd}$ grade ELA class could be better used to inspire and build lasting relationships that act as stepping stones to aid in a successful education.

The vibe was digital and independent, there was no time for nurturing, not in this class at least. Classroom management is every teacher's choice, and I respect that. The management of this particular class, the one which ultimately led to my son wanting to kill himself, could use some serious improvement, not the support of the administration.

I tell you all of this because I truly believe that there has been a shift in what is "normal", I don't think typical is normal any longer. I would challenge you to call around and find a few doctors who provide assessments for learning disabilities and ask how far out they are booking. What logic are we holding on to these days that would support the lack of inclusivity for all children?

*"He is focusing on the ceiling."*

My son suffers from General Anxiety Disorder. He is incredibly observant and aware of his surroundings. During the first few weeks of school, I received an email from his English Language Arts (ELA) teacher. It turned out that there was a dark spot on the ceiling tile in his classroom that was distracting him. The teacher informed me that they had to redirect him numerous times, and he kept asking about that spot, it was approximately six times. The teacher had grown frustrated by his fixation and felt the need to email me, clearly running out of ideas on how to successfully redirect him.

When my son got home, I asked him about it. 'Hey buddy, what was on the ceiling in ELA?' He told me he couldn't really tell because it was so high up, but it looked like a wasp nest. I replied, 'Well, that is scary. Did any wasps fly off, or did you see any movement?' We discussed this for a bit, and we came to the conclusion that if it had been a wasp nest, surely one would have taken flight. I agreed with his logic. Together, we decided that it was probably just a stain from when the ceiling tiles were being installed. He never brought it up to the teacher again.

If the ELA teacher had asked him what he thought it was and walked through that anxiety with him, in less than five minutes they could have come to the realization together that it was in fact safe, and all would have been well. That didn't happen, what did happen was my son lost a little bit of trust in this teacher. He had been punished for feeling scared and anxious. He was made to feel wrong for feelings beyond his control. This goes back to the ability to rationalize intrusive thoughts. In children this is not instinctual, it often is learned by adults to walk them through these moments and allow them to sort the thoughts out to conclude a realistic approach.

### *"He is always using the bathroom."*

Anxiety works in mysterious ways, and General Anxiety Disorder (GAD) exemplifies the complexity of this condition. Unlike specific anxieties triggered by known events or situations, GAD operates without a discernible cause, making it a constant, nagging presence in the lives of those affected. This ongoing anxiety, unrelated to any particular event, has a profound impact on daily life.

Individuals with GAD find themselves in a relentless cycle of worry, often fixating on improbable scenarios. Someone with GAD often does not remember the last time that they actually felt relaxed due to this constant anxiety which is ever-present within their psyche This persistent apprehension can disrupt even the most routine aspects of their day-to-day existence. The mind, consumed by constant anxiety, struggles to find moments of peace, hindering focus and concentration. Tasks that were once simple become monumental challenges, as the mind is preoccupied with a perpetual sense of panic.

Moreover, GAD doesn't merely manifest as psychological distress; it can also trigger a range of physical symptoms, showcasing the interconnectedness of mind and body. Hidden anxieties can manifest in various ways, such as stomach aches, muscle cramps, and tension. The body, responding to the ongoing stress, may succumb to frequent headaches, further adding to the burden carried by those with GAD. Even mundane bodily functions, like urination, can be affected, serving as a stark reminder of the pervasive nature of this disorder.

In essence, GAD encapsulates the profound impact anxiety can have on every facet of a person's life. It's not merely a fleeting worry or momentary unease; it's a relentless companion, disrupting mental peace and physical well-being. Understanding the multifaceted nature of GAD is crucial, as it highlights the importance of empathy, support, and effective coping strategies for those navigating this intricate web of anxiety.

Midway through the school year, the ELA teacher began emailing me about his frequent urination. I found out that the entire class would visit the bathroom together, and approximately 30 to 45 minutes later, he would ask to go again during class. The teacher expressed concern, citing that he was 'disrupting instruction.' I felt the term 'instruction' was used rather loosely in this context. Nevertheless, I inquired if he was misbehaving in the bathroom, spending excessive time outside the class, or if any misconduct was taking place. To my surprise, there were no issues reported.

At the beginning of the school year, the administration was informed about his medical diagnosis, and we struggled to establish a basic 504 plan.

This situation persisted for months, and I was not willing to instruct my child to stop using the bathroom. He informed me that he was losing his 'Dojos' for taking restroom breaks. Any reward points he earned were deducted for simply asking to use the restroom. Additionally, the teacher denied him access to water, while the rest of the class could drink freely. This denial of water was an attempt to control his fluid intake and minimize bathroom trips. If only someone had informed the teacher that such tactics were ineffective.

One day, my son came home deeply upset and humiliated. There was an issue with another teacher's computer during class, a teacher who happened to be his instructor the previous year. The ELA teacher proceeded to inquire about my son's bathroom habits in front of the entire class. They discussed his frequent bathroom usage in detail, leaving him feeling embarrassed and exposed. When this behavior was brought to their attention, they failed to acknowledge any wrongdoing.

He said that he didn't know what to do; he had to go, and he couldn't hold it. These urgent bathroom trips seemed to be confined to the ELA class. One day, I received an email from the teacher describing a bathroom 'emergency.' My heart sank as I realized my child was struggling, trying to ignore it and hold it in while being visibly uncomfortable.

When I received the 'emergency' email, I immediately called the doctor. I explained the situation and requested a urinalysis to rule out any infection or underlying physical condition that I might have missed. Within 25 minutes of receiving the email, I arrived at the school and took him straight to the doctor. To my relief, the urinalysis came back perfect; he had no infections. The doctor reiterated how GAD worked and firmly stated that this was a problem with the teacher, not the child.

I composed an email to the team including the principal, counselor, and the superintendent. I explained the results of the tests that were run, and the doctor's opinion. I went on to list the various confirmed actions that had been taken by the ELA teacher in an effort to stop frequent urination and how none of them were appropriate or effective. I said that punishment for bathroom usage was not appropriate and that it was not a privilege that they had any right to revoke. I told my son that if he was put in a position where he was not allowed to go he had my permission to walk out and go. In my mind, the humiliation that would come from having an accident was not worth it. I told the teacher that perhaps their reaction to the bathroom requests was more distracting than just letting him go. After all, we are preaching independence, right?

My son is not comfortable showing skin. When he was a baby, he would often be found in just a diaper, I thought he would grow up to be a free spirit. However, as he got older, he became very self-aware and refused to be shirtless even at the pool. Going for a physical at the doctor's office is a challenge; he doesn't want anyone looking at his tummy. There was even an incident with a mole, where we had to cover the entire area except for the tiny mole. I respect his feelings and boundaries completely. He has every right to feel this way about his body, and it's essential to honor his comfort level, as it is his body after all. Who am I to say that he should feel a certain way?

I bring all of this up because, while we were eating dinner one night, he casually said something in passing that caught our attention. We were talking about how school was going and if he was still being punished for going to the bathroom. He told us that he was, and they had tried to enforce a sign-out sheet for him to use every time, but he didn't care. He didn't care because he was able to go to the bathroom without being watched. "Excuse me?" I asked him to elaborate, I wanted to know who was watching him and when he was being watched.

He said that when they did their bathroom breaks as a class the ELA teacher would come in and watch the boys. He said that when he would walk out, they would stop watching and go back out into the hall with the rest of the class. I asked if the girls had ever been watched. "No, just the boys". I asked if the teacher would announce themselves before coming in. "No".

The ELA teacher is female and while there was also a male teacher in the 3$^{rd}$ grade and right next door; the male teacher was never called to monitor bathroom usage. None of the other teachers in any of the other classes he had would watch the children use the restroom. He said that she would watch him in the mirror sometimes if the bathroom layout was different than their normal one. He was extremely aware that she was watching him, and he clearly didn't like it.

It all made sense. I felt horrible. I had seen the fight this child put up for a mole at the Doctor's office and now he was being punished for wanting to go to the bathroom alone without being watched. He was probably rushing through and not getting it all out so he could get out of there. This is why he would go to the bathroom alone during class. This was rushing through my head all at once. How did I miss this? I never even thought to ask him about his comfort level during the group bathroom breaks.

Non-touching abuse is indeed a form of abuse, and according to North Carolina law, actions such as watching a child undress or use the bathroom qualify as sexual abuse. When I took my son to his therapist, he openly shared every detail of what he had told us at dinner without hesitation, and without missing a single detail. The therapist was equally disturbed by the information, underscoring the seriousness of the situation.

When my husband and I had our virtual meeting with the superintendent we brought this up as something that was incredibly inappropriate. The superintendent had no response to what we just told them. NOT A WORD. They sat there as if they were just waiting for me to stop talking. Nothing was ever addressed by the school regarding the sexual abuse. I hate that I missed it and was not able to help him. This poor child was being punished for not being okay with it.

I feel it necessary to explain that it is not the victim's job to try and understand the intentions of the abuser. The feelings that come from someone else's actions as it pertains to sexual abuse are real. We teach our kids that they get to say what happens to their bodies. We as parents approve select individuals that are "ok". Doctors, teachers, mommies, and daddies are usually deemed safe for kids. Where is that line, and why does it seem farther away when it comes to children? How can a school ignore the feelings a child has and the behavior of an adult, who should know better? This teacher took advantage of a child, and because of their job title, it was overlooked and allowed. Because the school's superintendents' arrogance and negligence were permitted.

*"His iPad is never charged."*

Technology is a requirement these days so naturally schools have adopted the use within the classroom and rightfully so as the world is not slowing down in the embrace of a digital presence. Kids should be comfortable with the ins and outs and learn to navigate various forms of technology, I get it. I had a hard time navigating through their programs so I can imagine a child having a hard time. Parents are told to go to the Schoology app, click the teacher's bit Moji, and click the chalkboard, it has the assignments for the day, but make sure you click it for the links. My head spins and I get overwhelmed. Every subject was on this iPad, and if on the off chance he had a paper or a project, he was to take a photo of it and upload it to whatever platform the teacher had instructed.

I work in a corporate job, and often technology is not on our side. When my internet won't start up, or my laptop is not charged fully, or I get thrown into an update and can't do anything at no point would I lose my job over it. I am an adult and I have fewer repercussions for failed technology than my son had in his third-grade ELA class. Is this level of "independence" the ELA teacher pushes truly for the kids, or is it designed to benefit the teacher?

The kids are expected to plug their devices into a charging cart when they are done and that is where they stay until they use them again. Along with the many, many emails about his bathroom use I also received them about his iPad not being charged. "Today his iPad was dead, could not participate". "He didn't charge the iPad and it died". "Behind on work because his iPad was not charged". While I understood where the teacher was coming from to a point, I had to ask if there was something wrong with the iPad or the charger itself. I know personally I go through several chargers a year. Was he not plugging it in all the way? My son swore up and down he would plug it in every time. When I was told that it was 100% his fault and not a technical issue, I went on to ask if the teachers checked the cart at the end of the day to make sure the kids had them in the chargers all the way.

I failed to see the harm in the teacher taking a quick glance inside the cart at the end of the day, just to ensure everything was in order. However, it became apparent that this was not within their job description, and the independence argument resurfaced. Undeterred, I decided to stand my ground.

I voiced my concerns, saying, 'Let me make sure I understand this correctly. You have a child with diagnosed issues that hinder their ability to focus in the way you expect. This child has Generalized Anxiety Disorder and frequently feels overwhelmed. As a result, they are struggling in class, and in the unfortunate event that their iPads are dead, they are left with nothing to do because you can't or won't provide paper copies. At what point do you step in to support the child?' Once again, the response echoed the independence argument.

This issue lasted most of the year. There were 504 accommodations that were designed for this ELA teacher to provide a checklist on Fridays so that we could log on at home and help him get caught up. The post-it notes with assignments and no context scribbled on them came home twice throughout the whole year.

I might be out of line by asking, what it was that this ELA teacher actually did. Hell, the iPad programs graded the assignments for them. YouTube conducted class story time and building relationships clearly didn't take too much of their time.

Every day this teacher would send home something negative to say, and I started to ignore it. The feeling of not being good enough was taking over, I could see how defeated my son was getting. I expressed to the teacher how he felt. I told them during a conference that he needed some positivity, and I tried to explain it in various ways that the teacher would understand.

Needless to say, what I expressed was only making it worse for him. The teacher didn't take a single thing to heart, in fact, it became worse. It was almost as the communication alone was enough for them to hold a grudge. The teacher just stopped communicating with me altogether, it would take me two or three attempts to engage through email and the 504 meetings apparently became optional, when they stopped showing up to them.

This behavior was not isolated to my son, it later came out that the reputation this particular ELA teacher had was not a positive one. Things you never know when you're in the thick of it. The idea that you might not be alone, is always a reflective thought.

I met with the principal several times and they refused to discuss the teacher unless they were present; I was told it was the school's policy. If the teacher's name came up, they would need to be present for the conversation, and that would involve another meeting.

I pushed back and asked the principal at what point they would intervene in the negative behavior of their staff and actually manage the situation. The principal just stared at me, and finally, they said, "That is not my role".

### *"The Red Communication Folder"*

The struggle for a solid 504 plan was real at this school, what we needed was an IEP, but they ignored that request. While we were climbing the constant uphill battle for an equal education opportunity, we also took in three children. Yep, we were fostering three children who had been removed from their homes by the state. They were my nieces and nephews. Things were crazy as you can imagine, and the three children came from a seriously traumatic home. So, it was even more important that I maintain a sense of calm.

The Charter school we attended was done on a lotto system, so getting these kids in was not going to happen. Though, if we are being honest, I would have rather poured honey in my ears and took a nap on a fire ant hill, than to have this fight with this school times three.

This is relevant because they were enrolled in our "zoned" public school. I was able to see what both sides of the spectrum were like. We got to experience public and charter schools simultaneously. During a meeting at the public school, the counselor created a behavior/communication chart. It was perfect for this child; I was so impressed. These kids had been at this school for a week and the team had already come together for no other reason than to touch base. I had been asking for two months at the charter school for a 504 meeting, on an existing 504 plan.

The behavior chart was essentially there to follow the child throughout the day, during her classes, and even during specials. The teachers would make notes, we could track the time of day when she would start to act out, it really was genius. We could track her triggers and in turn, develop coping skills and interventions.

I took this folder and modified it a tad bit to meet the needs of my son. I ran back to the charter school with it, where they reluctantly adopted it. The form was modified again by the counselor to match our son's class blocks. The team made it very clear that he was to keep up with it, and the "independence advocate" aka, the ELA teacher made it clear that it was his responsibility, and they would not assist in helping him in the slightest keep up with it.

I wanted to see where the disconnect was. The folder was designed to show what work he was missing, allow for communication between parents and teachers as well as determine trends for triggers and his behaviors. The folder became nothing more than a place for the ELA teacher to nag about something. Every day was something negative. There was never anything he did well, nothing was celebrated, and the incomplete assignments were hardly ever noted. There were days at a time when the folder would go missing, only to magically turn up somewhere in the ELA teacher's possession.

It got to the point where I stopped even going over the folder with my son. The scratchy handwriting made little to no sense and lacked context, or it was the same complaint as yesterday. No interventions were ever applied to try and yield a different outcome. It meant nothing to him; it was just more of what he was not doing well. That feeling of not being good enough was starting to consume him. I could see his desire start to fade. This child had goals, he wanted to be on the honor roll. Slowly he stopped caring, he stopped expecting to be good enough for recognition. He was losing his spark, and I was not about to help expedite that process because his teacher could not find ONE thing that he did well. I didn't need to relay that message at home after he had to deal with it all day.

I tried so hard, it felt like I was praising things I knew were below his potential just to give him a boost. If he had the confidence, he would have surpassed many of the expectations set before him.

All that I asked for was communication, I didn't ask for the answers just an opportunity to talk about it. It was becoming abundantly clear that they didn't intend on actually trying to make this work for him.

After all of this, we left the school, we would be crazy not to. We went to the public school we were zoned for and the same one the other kids attended. We were blessed with a team that surrounded him with so much love and care. He wrapped his first quarter a few points shy of an A in ELA. This team watched him, and they made him feel like he was worth it and capable, and in return, he started to gain his spark back. He still had struggles, and he still had challenges, but sitting around a conference table, before school started talking about his 504-plan watching the counselor run through it on a big screen step by step was quite literally blowing my mind. While I know this is not the case for public schools across the board, it is how it should be. They had the idea that even though he faced challenges, he was smart and still had a wealth of knowledge they needed to get out of him. It was their job as educators to do it, they had the desire to do it.

While we are still dealing with the trauma of what that charter school left on him, we have made great strides. We talk about what was done to him, and we make sure he knows it was wrong. We validate his fears and are helping him trust again, it's a slow process but I am incredibly optimistic.

**"The Treasure Box is for positive reinforcement."**

The struggle with maintaining focus is an experience that many individuals can empathize with. It's important to recognize that the inability to stay focused is not a matter of choice; it's a challenging and often frustrating aspect of life. Despite the genuine desire to concentrate and complete tasks, the mind sometimes seems to have a will of its own, making it difficult to sustain attention.

I can relate to those moments when, despite your best efforts, you find yourself staring blankly at someone, unable to retain a single word of what they're saying. It can be incredibly frustrating to wish for the ability to follow instructions effortlessly and process the sequence of tasks seamlessly. There are occasions when you manage to do it, but unfortunately, it's not a consistent experience.

The longing for improvement and the ability to navigate through these challenges is genuine. It's a journey that requires patience, self-awareness, and understanding. It's admirable that you have reached a point of acceptance and are learning to cope with these struggles. It's a testament to your resilience and determination, especially considering that it took nearly thirty years to become aware of this challenge and find ways to navigate through it.

Remember, you are not alone in this journey, and there are strategies and support systems available to help you manage these difficulties. Stay strong, stay persistent, and keep believing in your ability to overcome these obstacles.

I went to pick my son up for a doctor's appointment early one day. While still in the parking lot, I said "How as school buddy". I heard a sigh, and I looked back. I was having flashbacks to the week prior when he said he didn't want to live … My stomach instantly knotted up. I see tears in his eyes, and his lip starts to quiver and get tight.

"I didn't get the treasure box today". I asked him, "why". He went on to tell me that it was for kids who could "focus" on their assignments and get work done. That was not an answer he would have said, this was told to him. I asked him to elaborate. He and another student who also has known and disclosed various diagnoses were made to sit and watch the entire class get called up to select a toy out of the treasure box. This was during the end-of-the-year mock EOG practice tests. These two boys were in testing accommodation and the methods of practice did not apply as they would not be taking the test in this format or in this location.

One by one, the class got their names called, and he had to sit there and wait for his turn. Unfortunately, his turn never came. Not that it mattered in the slightest, but I asked him if he had completed the assignment. He replied, 'I tried, but I didn't have enough time.' This was also in his 504 plan – to chunk up his work, yet another accommodation the school neglected.

I turned around in my seat, now facing him, still sitting in the parking lot. He was telling me he didn't cry in class; he held his tears back. I was boiling, fighting back the urge to walk right back into the school. I asked what the other little boy did when he realized he wasn't getting a prize. 'He just put his head down on the desk,' he said. I know this little boy well, and that made it hurt so much more.

This came about a week after my son expressed wanting to kill himself. I wrote an email to the principal and the teacher. I emailed the ELA teacher, not because I didn't believe my son, but because I had to confirm that this was actually happening. it was confirmed; in fact, I was told that "the rewards are for kids who can focus and get their assignments done".

I explained to my son in the parking lot of the school before we pulled out that this teacher was wrong for what they did. I had been at the dollar store earlier that day and happened to get a couple of little fidgets for him. I used them and kept them in my purse for those moments when we needed a distraction. I pulled one out of my purse and said, "Well, screw that teacher" and I handed my son the little fidget toy. His face lit up and he wiped his eyes and a smile appeared.

I took this opportunity again and reminded him that telling me his feelings was a good thing. I told him that we won't always be able to make people do the right thing and that sometimes we have to just ignore their ignorance. I let him know that he was justified in having feelings that made him sad and that he was right to talk about them.

This is a touchy subject because while I believe the challenges that he faces daily are a reason, they are not an excuse. I still am a firm believer in accountability, though that comes in the form of communication in my son's case.

We finally buckled up and went on our way. As I drove, my mind was racing, and my blood pressure was inching up and up. How on God's green earth could anyone be okay with what had happened, let alone be the one to do it? How can you sit and watch a child's heartbreak like that? To this day, I don't understand; I will never get it. We are supposed to protect our kids, but how can we do this when our teachers are the ones hurting them? I often don't think of a best-case scenario; I think of the worst and work my way up from there. I started to think about the kids who don't talk to their parents like my son does or the kids who physically can't talk.

We had our meeting with the superintendent a few days after this, and, of course, we brought this up as well. The superintendent said that the treasure box was a poor example and went on to say that it was meant to be used as positive reinforcement. I interrupted them and snapped, 'He has a known disability,' and they responded, 'What kind of disability makes him not finish his work?' I feel it necessary to remind everyone that this individual has a master's certification in special education.

I am literally at a loss at this point. This teacher can do no wrong. Jesus, how is this happening? What am I missing? Am I out of line?

At this point, many things were in motion and I had to bite my tongue. I was learning about grievance processes and filing the necessary complaints, so these meetings were merely a box to be checked on our end. Though they all were audio recorded, in many states you don't have to inform the other party that you are recording them. North Carolina is a one-party consent state.

These people didn't care, and I needed to stop expecting them to. My son's life was not worth it to them, and I could never say or do anything to change their mind.

I was the villain; I always would be. It went so far beyond just an education; they were robbing him of his potential. They stole his joy and were breaking him, slowly, day by day. I tend to expect the best in people, and when they not only fall short but manage to hurt others in the process, I feel a personal responsibility to make them see the error in their ways. It can often feel like a game of tug of war with the devil himself. My hands will bleed before I let go. The one thing I wish I knew at the beginning was everything I know now.

I could go on and on about the various examples of irrational and unethical behavior we experienced from the staff at this school, which ultimately shattered my son; but I want to avoid this book turning into a diatribe of tattles. I see it as much more beneficial to validate others and inspire them to stand up and speak, even when they think no one is listening.

"Our lives begin to end the day we become silent about things that matter."

– Martin Luther King JR.

# CHAPTER 9
# IEP/504

In 1975, Congress enacted the Education for All Handicapped Children Act (EHA), also known as EHA. This groundbreaking legislation was designed to provide crucial support to states and localities, aiming to protect the rights, meet the needs, and improve outcomes for youth with disabilities. The EHA marked a significant milestone in the realm of education by ensuring that children with disabilities were no longer denied access to education, granting them the opportunity to learn and thrive in an inclusive environment.

However, it was not until 1990 that the EHA underwent a transformation, evolving into the Individuals with Disabilities Education Act (IDEA). This reformation further strengthened the commitment to providing quality education for children with disabilities. In 2004, the IDEA saw revisions and the introduction of new regulations, enhancing its implementation and interpretation across the nation. These amendments aimed to refine the support systems and resources available to students, teachers, and parents, ensuring that the objectives of the act were met effectively.

The impact of IDEA on the educational landscape cannot be overstated. In the 2020-21 school year alone, an impressive 7.5 million children benefited from related services tailored to meet their individual needs. Furthermore, statistics revealed that more than 66% of these children were integrated into general education settings for over 80% of their school day. This encouraging data showcased the strides made in fostering an inclusive learning environment for all students, regardless of their abilities.

However, despite the positive strides, challenges persist, especially for parents navigating the complex educational landscape, particularly in schools like charter schools. For parents whose children are struggling, understanding the available programs and support mechanisms is crucial. Unfortunately, many charter schools similar to ours often fall short of providing comprehensive information and assistance to parents. This lack of transparency and support can be immensely frustrating, leaving parents feeling overwhelmed and underserved.

It is important to recognize that the issues faced by parents in charter schools are not unique to this specific educational model. Since IDEA is a federal act, its regulations and provisions apply universally, transcending school types. The challenges faced in accessing accurate information and appropriate support can be encountered in various educational settings across the country.

In light of these challenges, it becomes imperative for parents and guardians to advocate for their children effectively. This may involve seeking guidance from educational advocacy groups, connecting with other parents facing similar situations, and staying informed about their rights under IDEA. By empowering themselves with knowledge and support, parents can navigate the complexities of the educational system, ensuring that their children receive the quality education they deserve.

Schools receive funding based on the number of students enrolled, and additional funds are allocated for students with specific categorizations. For instance, in North Carolina during the 2022-2023 school year, the state provides an extra $5,275.72 for each student with an Individualized Education Program (IEP) in grades K-12. Despite this additional funding, our charter school claimed they lacked resources to provide simple accommodations like alternative seating, which could be as basic as an extra desk. This situation raises questions about how schools allocate their supplementary income.

If you notice your child is struggling with various day-to-day tasks, then it might be worth looking into. There are two programs both very different, and both have their own set of rules and expectations.

## CHAPTER 10:
# 504

All students who have an identified disability and/or impairment that substantially limits one or more major life activities are entitled to a Section 504 Accommodation Plan. Unlike Individualized Education Programs (IEPs), which are enforced at the state level, 504 plans are overseen by the Office of Civil Rights (OCR) at the federal level. Any complaints related to a 504 plan should be directed to the OCR; sending them through the state level may result in dismissal due to insufficiency.

Section 504 plans encompass a range of accommodations, including physical adjustments like ramps to facilitate access to specific areas of the school, as well as academic accommodations. For instance, a student with ADHD might be given the opportunity to take tests in a separate room to minimize distractions or receive extra time to complete exams. These 'accommodations' are designed to ensure that a student's disability does not hinder their participation in the school environment or access to the curriculum, bringing them on par with their non-disabled peers.

While IEPs generally offer more legal protection than 504 plans, it's important not to be discouraged by this distinction and still pursue the Section 504 process.

The process to obtain a diagnosis for these conditions is often lengthy and can be quite costly. In my experience, many psychologists I contacted had waiting lists spanning six to eight months. Moreover, insurance coverage for this type of testing is often limited, leaving you to cover the expenses out of pocket. The average cost can vary significantly, ranging from $800 to $1500. It's crucial to understand that having a formal diagnosis is not a prerequisite for obtaining a 504 plan.

Certainly, it's worth initiating the diagnostic process. I recommend exploring insurance-approved providers and being prepared for a wait, as gaining a deeper understanding of your child's challenges can empower you to better support them. However, it's important to note that a formal diagnosis is not mandatory to provide the necessary assistance your child requires.

When the teachers are emailing you, behaviors are becoming frequent, assignments are getting lost or forgotten and the child is clearly struggling, make the call. Get the team together and request a 504 meeting. Put it in writing and clearly state you would like a 504 plan, make sure to CC the entire team. The following is an example to work off of, it does not need to be exact, though the more details you include the less they can argue that you didn't.

*Dear Principal:*

*I request that my students be evaluated to determine if they are eligible to receive accommodations under a 504 Plan. I believe my student may be eligible because they (check all that apply):*

*\_\_\_\_ Have been diagnosed with the following disability:*

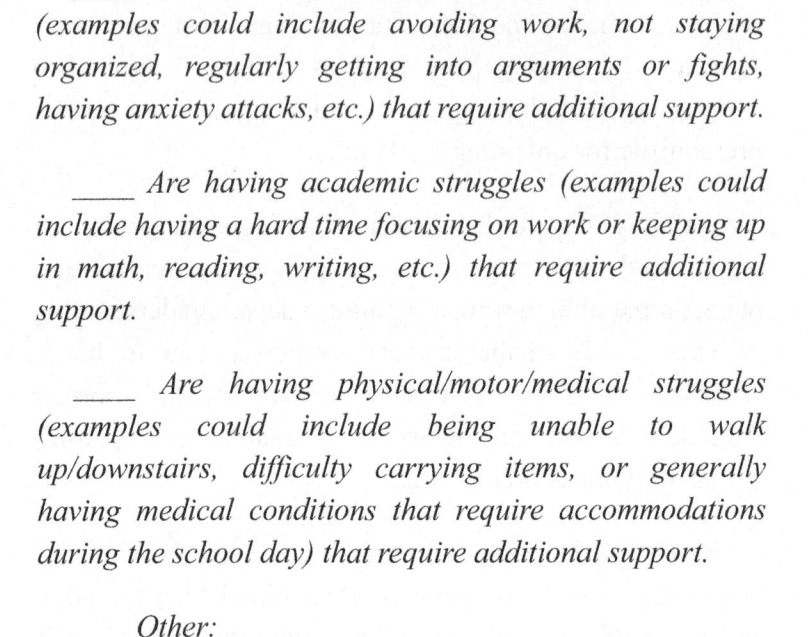

____ Are having behavioral/emotional struggles (examples could include avoiding work, not staying organized, regularly getting into arguments or fights, having anxiety attacks, etc.) that require additional support.

____ Are having academic struggles (examples could include having a hard time focusing on work or keeping up in math, reading, writing, etc.) that require additional support.

____ Are having physical/motor/medical struggles (examples could include being unable to walk up/downstairs, difficulty carrying items, or generally having medical conditions that require accommodations during the school day) that require additional support.

____ Other: _____

Please contact me within 10 school days to schedule a time to meet with you to discuss the process and for me to sign any necessary paperwork so that my child's needs can be addressed as soon as possible. Also, please accept this request as written consent to evaluate my child.

Thank you.

If the school complies and fulfills your request, that's great. However, if they do not, it's crucial to maintain a paper trail, which you'll need when filing a formal complaint. The purpose of these programs is to ensure equal education for all children, so don't let the school persuade you otherwise. Writing your request in a clear and precise manner will demonstrate your understanding of the process, potentially reducing any bureaucratic runaround.

After last year, my new favorite term is 'paper trail.' It has been my lifeline throughout this experience. If you don't already have one, create a timeline document while the dates and events are fresh in your mind. Keep it updated, so you can easily reference any details during this process. Living in a constant state of defense isn't ideal, but our charter school left me no choice. It's better to be assertive than passive when it comes to our children, as not everyone shares the same interests.

The school does have the right to deny a request for a 504 plan, stating they don't find it necessary. In such cases, a new process unfolds, often outlined in the school's handbook regarding the steps to dispute this decision. It's important that they provide information about their appeals process if your request for reevaluation is denied.

If this situation arises, consider consulting the child's pediatrician before requesting a second evaluation. The pediatrician can offer a diagnosis and referral swiftly. Although the pediatrician may not delve deeply into the child's learning challenges or pinpoint the exact level of the spectrum they fall under, they are familiar with your child and can advocate for them. Use this referral and resubmit your request along with the letter. Allow the school to deny the request once more. You may choose to pursue this option even before making the initial request; the decision is yours to make.

If they do tell you no or refer you to their appeals process, do it. you will most likely be looking at what is referred to as "due process". It is basically a mediation process with a $3^{rd}$ party, and you will be able to present the areas of concern that led you to the initial request. You can present your pediatrician's referral as well as any supporting documents. I would prepare grade reports, teachers' emails, and student work samples.

It is very important to note that the school is also responsible for acknowledging the needs and struggles a child presents with. There are federal regulations that require and hold the school responsible for noticing areas of concern; we will discuss that in more detail later.

There are dedicated IEP/504 Advocates available to assist you throughout this process. These advocates specialize in crafting accommodations, providing guidance, and even attending meetings with the school on your behalf. They are there to work in your best interests and advocate for your child. With their expertise in the process, their services typically range from $200 to $400 per hour, and in many cases, their assistance proves invaluable. To find one in your area, simply search for 'IEP/504 Advocate' online. Most advocates offer a free fifteen-minute consultation to discuss your situation. However, knowing what you need and want is beneficial, there are Facebook groups for moms for children with special needs. There are some that are specific to IEP and 504s, ask all the questions. Many of them have been where you are. The Advocate while a great resource and can provide great guidance. I am writing this book to help those who don't have unlimited resources, that should never be a reason you can't help your child.

In an ideal scenario, the school complies with your request, and a meeting is scheduled. Typically, the attendees include you, the teachers, the counselor, and usually the principal or assistant principal. During the meeting, a formal 504 form will be used as a reference, and you will receive a copy along with an explanation of your rights. The discussions will revolve around the observations from both teachers and you regarding the child's behavior in class and at home. The objective is to bridge the gap between home and school, with everyone working together collaboratively. Think of it as an 'all hands on deck' approach. The team will share basic ideas and suggest strategies to address the challenges your child is facing. The process should be constructive, and you should ideally leave the meeting feeling confident. After the meeting, the agreed-upon accommodations should be implemented promptly.

There will be some that work and some that don't. The team should be open to communication, so you will know what is working and what is not, and remember that it's a trial and error for you and the teachers alike. This is an open stage for communication and not every case is ideal. The requirement is for one meeting annually, though you can call as many meetings as often as you need. I would follow the same style in your 504-plan meeting request as the initial request, providing clear details as to what you want to discuss.

*Dear Principal:*

*I would like to meet with my student's 504 Plan Team to discuss my student's: (Check all that apply.)*

*_____ My student is having behavioral struggles (examples could include avoiding work, not staying organized, regularly getting into arguments or fights, etc.) that aren't being met by their 504 Plan.*

_____ My student is having academic struggles (examples could include having a hard time keeping up in math, reading, writing, etc.) that aren't being met by their 504 Plan.

_____ My student needs new or different accommodations (examples could include extended time on tests, opportunities for sensory breaks, chunked assignments, etc.) to meet their needs.

_____ My student needs a functional behavioral assessment (FBA) and behavior intervention plan (BIP) to help address ongoing behavior needs.

_____ Other: _____

Additional information:

Please have someone contact me within 10 school days with a possible date, time, and location for a 504

Team meeting.

Thank you,

It does not always work like this; our charter school was a nightmare and barely adhered to its own minimal suggested accommodations. It was not until we changed schools that I was speechless when I learned and saw firsthand how this should be handled. The living document, that timeline is where you will want to keep track of what works and what doesn't and how you communicated those concerns. The school can also be held accountable for failure to adhere to the 504 plans but again, you will need clear-cut documentation proving that be the case. The documentation is usually by email, try and keep those communications in writing.

Many states are like North Carolina in that they are a one-party consent state, which means you don't need their consent to record them. You also don't need to disclose that you are recording them. On Amazon you can get a tiny little recorder for 34 dollars, it works great. Then you can upload the files to the computer and have any communications saved for a rainy day.

This is exhausting, though the idea is that the more parents that are comfortable holding these schools accountable and knowing their rights and are ready for anything, the less likely the schools will try and pull their shit.

You may feel that the 504 is not working, or perhaps you feel that the level of accommodations needed is much more in line with what the IEP can provide, you may request that assessment at any time as well. Sometimes behaviors will surface, and an intervention plan is needed or requested.

I was told by our charter school that you cannot run these interventions simultaneously. That was a lie. I spoke with an advocate myself and learned that I could get an FBA and BIP while having a 504 and while waiting for an IEP assessment. I don't want to get in the weeds on this yet, I just don't want you to feel stuck if you think this 504 is not working. If you feel this way, then you need to ask for what you need, just do it in writing. You will keep what you have in place until the next intervention is implanted, should you go from 504 to an IEP.

We filed a formal complaint because our school failed to comply with an IEP request. The school took full advantage of the indirect communications and paired that with a subjective and false statement written by their attorney. The school was found to be "in compliance". This complaint was not in our favor because I did not clearly stay the course in my request. I actually thought that the school knew best, and I trusted them. The NCDPI acknowledged that it could have been read another way, yet the decision was final.

# CHAPTER 11
# IEP

An Individualized Education Program (IEP) is a tailored plan designed to provide specialized education and related services to a child with a qualifying disability. This crucial educational framework is established under the federal law known as the Individuals with Disabilities Education Act (IDEA). The IEP process begins when someone initiates a written request to evaluate whether a child qualifies for these specialized services.

Distinguishing the IEP from the 504 plan reveals a nuanced landscape. While both mechanisms aim to support students with disabilities, they operate under different regulations and frameworks. Both have a different legibility criteria, development process and purpose.

The IEP is a comprehensive and legally binding document that outlines an individualized strategy to address a student's unique needs. It includes specific academic goals, measurable objectives, and details about the services and accommodations the student will receive. The IEP process involves a collaborative effort between parents, educators, and other relevant professionals, fostering a team approach to meeting the student's educational requirements.

On the other hand, the 504 plan is rooted in Section 504 of the Rehabilitation Act of 1973, which prohibits discrimination against individuals with disabilities. Unlike the IEP, a 504 plan doesn't require the same level of individualized academic goals or specialized services. Instead, it focuses on removing barriers to ensure equal access for students with disabilities. This may involve accommodations such as changes to the physical environment, adjustments in teaching methods, or additional support services.

| | IEP | 504 |
|---|---|---|
| Basic description | A blueprint or plan for a child's special education experience at school. | A blueprint or plan for how the school will provide support and remove barriers for a student with a disability. |
| What it does | Provides individualized special education and related services to meet a child's unique needs. These services are provided at no cost to families. | Provides services and changes to the learning environment to enable students to learn alongside their peers. As with an IEP, a 504 plan is provided at no cost to families. |
| What law applies | The Individuals with Disabilities Education Act (IDEA): This is a federal special education law for children with disabilities. | Section 504 of the Rehabilitation Act of 1973: This is a federal civil rights law to stop discrimination against people with disabilities. |
| Who's eligible | To get an IEP, there are two requirements: A child has one or more of the 13 disabilities listed in IDEA. The law lists specific challenges, like learning disabilities, ADHD, autism, and others. And the disability must affect the child's educational performance and/or ability to learn and benefit from the general education curriculum. The child must need specialized instruction to make progress in school. | To get a 504 plan, there are two requirements: A child has any disability. Section 504 covers a wide range of different struggles in school. **And** the disability must interfere with the child's ability to learn in a general education classroom. Section 504 has a broader definition of a disability than IDEA. (It says a disability must substantially limit one or more basic life activities. This can include learning, reading, communicating, and thinking.) That's why a child who doesn't qualify for an IEP might still be able to get a 504 plan. |
| Independent educational evaluation | Families can ask the school district to pay for an independent educational evaluation (IEE) by an outside expert. The district doesn't have to agree. Families can always pay for an outside evaluation themselves, but the district may not give it much weight. | Doesn't allow families to ask for an IEE. As with an IEP evaluation, families can always pay for an outside evaluation themselves. |
| Who creates it | There are strict legal requirements about who participates. With a few exceptions, the entire IEP team must be present for IEP meetings. The team must include:<br>• The child's parent or caregiver<br>• At least one of the child's general education teachers<br>• At least one special education teacher<br>• A school psychologist or other specialist who can interpret evaluation results<br>• A district representative with authority over special education services | The rules about who's on the 504 team are less specific than they are for an IEP. A 504 plan is created by a team of people who are familiar with the child and who understand the evaluation data and special services options. This might include:<br>• The child's parent or caregiver<br>• General and special education teachers<br>• The school principal |
| What's in it | The IEP sets learning goals and describes the services the school will provide. It's a written document. Here are some of the most important things the IEP must include:<br>• The child's present levels of academic and functional performance — how the child is currently doing in school<br>• Annual education goals for the child and how the school will track progress<br>• The services the child will get — this may include special education, related, supplementary, and extended school year services<br>• The timing of services — when they start, how often they occur, and how long they last<br>• Any accommodations — changes to the child's learning environment<br>• Any modifications — changes to what the child is expected to learn or know<br>• How the child will participate in standardized tests<br>• How the child will be included in general education classes and school activities | There is no standard 504 plan. Unlike an IEP, a 504 plan doesn't have to be a written document. A 504 plan generally includes the following:<br>• Specific accommodations, supports, or services for the child<br>• Names of who will provide each service<br>• Name of the person responsible for ensuring the plan is implemented |

| | IEP | 504 |
|---|---|---|
| Notice | When the school wants to change a child's services or placement, it has to tell families in writing before the change. This is called **prior written notice**. Notice is also required for any IEP meetings and evaluations. Families also have "stay put" rights to keep services in place while there's a disagreement about the IEP. | The school must notify families about an evaluation or a "significant change" in placement. Notice doesn't have to be in writing, but most schools do so anyway. |
| Consent | A parent or caregiver must consent in writing for the school to evaluate a child. They must also consent in writing before the school can provide the services in an IEP. | A parent or caregiver's consent is required for the school district to evaluate a child. |
| How often it's reviewed and revised | The IEP team must review the IEP at least once a year. The child must be reevaluated every three years to determine whether services are still needed. | The rules vary by state. Generally, a 504 plan is reviewed each year and a reevaluation is done every three years or when needed. |
| How to resolve disputes | IDEA gives families several ways to resolve disputes (usually in this order):<br>• Mediation<br>• Due process complaint<br>• Resolution session<br>• Civil lawsuit<br>• State complaint<br>• Lawsuit | Section 504 gives families several options for resolving disagreements with the school:<br>• Mediation<br>• Alternative dispute resolution<br>• Impartial hearing<br>• Complaint to the Office for Civil Rights (OCR)<br>• Lawsuit |
| Funding/costs | Students receive these services at no charge. States receive additional funding for students with IEPs. | Students receive these services at no charge. States do not receive extra funding for students with 504 plans. But the federal government can take funding away from programs (including schools) that don't meet their legal duty to serve kids with disabilities. IDEA funds can't be used to serve students with 504 plans. |

In essence, the IEP is more robust and prescriptive, providing a detailed roadmap for a student's academic journey, while the 504 plan is a flexible tool aimed at eliminating barriers to ensure equal educational opportunities. Section 504 is broader and focuses on equal access, while an IEP provides more intensive and specialized educational services for students who meet specific eligibility criteria. Understanding the distinctions between these two crucial frameworks is pivotal for parents, educators, and administrators alike, as it enables them to better advocate for and support students with diverse learning needs.

In the initial phase of the Individualized Education Program (IEP) process, known as the "Referral" stage, it is imperative that any request for an IEP assessment be formally submitted in writing. This Referral can be instigated by various stakeholders, including parents, legal guardians, teachers, principals, vice-principals, guidance counselors, teacher's assistants, or any other school employee equipped with pertinent information about the child's functioning within the school environment.

Once the Referral letter is submitted to the principal, a critical timeline is set into motion. By law, this timeline spans a duration of 90 days, measured in calendar days rather than solely school days. It's important to note that a standard school year typically comprises 180 days. Therefore, the 90-day timeline represents a significant portion of the academic year, underlining the urgency and importance of prompt action in the IEP evaluation process.

This timeframe is designed to ensure swift and efficient responses to the identified needs of the student. It emphasizes the commitment to timely assessment and intervention, acknowledging the crucial role that time plays in a child's academic and developmental progress.

During this 90-day period, the school system is mandated to conduct a thorough assessment, collaborate with relevant stakeholders, and develop an Individualized Education Program that aptly addresses the unique needs of the student in question. This commitment to a relatively swift turnaround underscores the gravity of recognizing and meeting the educational requirements of students with qualifying disabilities.

The 90-day timeline serves as a legal framework to safeguard the rights of students with disabilities, ensuring that the IEP process proceeds with diligence and expediency to provide timely and tailored support for each child's educational journey.

This means that by the 90th calendar day after the parent submits the written Referral, the following things must have happened:

1. The school must have evaluated the child.
2. The school must have held an IEP meeting that included the parent(s) to determine if the child is eligible for an IEP.
3. If the child is determined eligible for an IEP, the school must have written the IEP.

The 90-day timeline cannot be extended, even if requested it be extended.

Do not let a school kick the can down the road, they are very aware of the timelines and if they are like our charter school will take full advantage of it. Schools will often say that the 90-day timeline starts when the parent signs the paperwork giving permission for the school to begin evaluating or testing the child. That is not correct. IDEA specifically says that the timeline starts when the written referral is made, and the Referral is the written request by letter or email for evaluation, not the consent for evaluation.

The 90-day timeline applies even in summer and during breaks from school, like school holidays. For example, if a Referral letter or email is sent to the principal on June 1, the eligibility process, the 3 steps of evaluation, eligibility, and IEP—must be completed by August 29, 90 days from June 1. This is because the definition of "day" in Policies is calendar days, not school or business days.

Below is a sample of an IEP request, Legal Aid emphasizes the importance of dating the documentation, communications, and requests. Once you are done drafting your communications read it back to yourself as though it was being read by a third party. A third party does not know the background or prior events, so make sure that if there are any references to behaviors or actions include them.

*Principal:*

*School:*

*School Address:*

*Name of Town, NC Zip code [or principal's email address if sending by email]*

*Exceptional Children's Director:*

*County Schools Superintendent's Office Address:*

*Name of Town, NC Zip code [or EC Director's address if sending by email]*

*Date:*

*Regarding: Request for Evaluation for IEP under IDEA for [Student's Name]*

*Dear Principal _____ and EC Director _____:*

*I am writing about my child \_\_\_\_ who is in the \_\_\_\_ grade at your school. _____'s date of birth is _____.*

_____ is having significant trouble in school with _____. _____ needs help with _____.

I believe that my child may have a disability. I am requesting that the school evaluate my child for an IEP under IDEA.

I understand that the school has 90 calendar days from the date of this letter to evaluate my child, and if my child is found eligible, create my child's IEP. I understand that as the parent I am a member of the IEP team and will be involved in making decisions about my child's IEP.

I also understand that the IEP team will need to meet soon so that we can complete the Special Education Referral and Informed Consent for Evaluation forms. Please call me at _____ or email me at _____ to set the meeting time.

Thank you for your time.

Sincerely,

Parent's Name

After submitting the referral letter, you have the option to follow up a few days later to confirm its receipt, although this step is not obligatory. While it is not mandated, this proactive approach can provide you with reassurance and a sense of engagement in the IEP process. It's worth noting that navigating through the intricacies of the IEP journey can be complex, and there is assistance available to guide you. Remember, the IEP process involves collaboration between parents, educators, and other professionals to create a plan tailored to the individual needs of the student. Seeking assistance from a variety of sources can help you make informed decisions and ensure that your child receives the appropriate support in their education.

Despite the expectation that student handbooks should be accurate and easily accessible, this isn't always the case. Often, necessary edits and improvements stem from various complaints and grievances, particularly in charter schools. These institutions, while granted the autonomy to create their own content, are bound by state and federal statutes ensuring equal educational opportunities. In some instances, deficiencies in information may only be rectified after concerns are raised, as was the case with your charter school, prompting the belated inclusion of a brief description of state guidelines.

One valuable resource to navigate these challenges is the Exceptional Children's Assistance Center (ECAC). ECAC serves as a vital support system, offering webinars on diverse topics related to neurodivergence and the broader exceptional children (EC) community. Unfortunately, many parents only discover such resources after finding themselves overwhelmed with the complexities of the system. Despite your requests, it seems the school did not proactively educate parents about these resources.

Understanding that assistance is available empowers parents to advocate more effectively for their children. While the school may not have taken the initiative to provide this information, seeking out resources such as the ECAC. Recognizing and leveraging such resources can significantly contribute to a more informed and collaborative approach to addressing the unique needs of neurodivergent students and those in the exceptional children community.

# CHAPTER 12
# FBA

Kids exhibit specific behaviors for various reasons, often without a clear understanding of why they act the way they do. It is the responsibility of schools to delve into the root causes behind these behaviors and propose viable solutions. This investigative process is formally known as a Functional Behavior Assessment (FBA), a method focused on evaluating behavior. The primary objective of an FBA is to unravel the underlying factors contributing to behavioral challenges. By identifying these factors, educators and professionals can develop effective strategies to modify and improve the behavior. In engaging with the process of a Functional Behavior Assessment (FBA), educators collaborate closely with parents, caregivers, and, when applicable, the students themselves. This collaborative approach ensures a holistic understanding of the child's environment, triggers, and potential stressors. The information gathered through open communication contributes to a comprehensive FBA, enriching the analysis and strengthening the foundation for tailored interventions.

Children are unique individuals with their own emotions, preferences, and personalities. Despite this individuality, there tends to be a shroud of mystery surrounding the concept of "behaviors" in children. Consider how, as adults, we have certain coping mechanisms or ways of expressing ourselves. For instance, if an adult uses sarcasm to sidestep an emotional situation, it's generally accepted without much scrutiny. If an adult makes a mean-spirited comment, they may be labeled negatively, but life moves on. Unfortunately, children don't always have the luxury of fully expressing themselves in the structured environment of a school.

An interesting perspective on this matter comes from an article challenging adults to experience a role reversal with their children during a shopping trip. The experiment involved adults refraining from touching or asking for anything, essentially putting themselves in the position of a child. Imagine wandering through a store, sipping on a Starbucks, but not having the freedom to touch anything or suggest which aisle to explore. If you've ever tried this exercise, you likely gained valuable insights into the constraints and frustrations children might feel in similar situations.

The comparison underscores the importance of understanding and addressing the emotional needs of children in educational settings. Just as adults have coping mechanisms and ways of expressing themselves, children too need outlets for their emotions and a supportive environment that recognizes and accommodates their individuality. This recognition is at the heart of the FBA process, aiming to decode the motivations behind behavior and pave the way for constructive solutions that foster a more positive and understanding educational experience.

The request for an FBA needs to be done in writing, much like the 504 and IEP requests. The request can be made by the parents or the school at any time, just make sure it's done in writing.

The act of expressing oneself to alleviate emotional burdens is a universal need, and children encounter this challenge daily. Throughout the school day, kids are expected to sit in class and perform academically. However, it's crucial to acknowledge that each child brings their unique set of emotions and feelings to the classroom environment.

Certainly, children will be children, and occasional rule-breaking or lapses in judgment are part of the growing process. It is when these behaviors persist, manifesting as a pattern of disruptive actions, that intervention becomes necessary. Such behaviors not only pose challenges for the individual child but can also have a broader impact by disrupting the learning environment for other students.

These disruptive behaviors extend beyond the scope of commonly outlined neurodivergent behaviors. They encompass a range of actions, from becoming withdrawn and throwing objects to yelling, interrupting, tardiness, skipping class, cursing, acting out, and displaying general defiance. Recognizing and addressing these behaviors is crucial not only for the well-being of the individual child but also for maintaining a conducive and positive learning atmosphere for the entire classroom.

In light of these challenges, it becomes evident that a comprehensive and empathetic approach is needed to understand the root causes of such behaviors. This understanding is essential for educators and professionals to implement effective interventions and support systems tailored to the unique needs of each child. By acknowledging and addressing the emotional complexities that children bring to the school environment, we can foster an atmosphere where students feel heard, supported, and equipped to navigate the complexities of their emotions in a constructive manner. This, in turn, contributes to a more inclusive and conducive learning environment for all.

It is important that these requests are also in writing, while the school can initiate these FBAs as well, if you feel one needs to be conducted make sure you include the necessary information.

*Date:*

*Dear IEP Case Manager/Special Education Teacher or Principal*

*Re: Request for FBA*

*I am requesting a Functional Behavioral Assessment (FBA) for my child. [Add child's full name]*

*I am concerned that my child's behavior is interfering with their education. [Add more detail here, for example: they are not making progress on IEP goals, or it is keeping them from spending more time in general education.]*

*I am also requesting an IEP team (or 504 team) meeting to discuss a plan for the FBA. [Make a note here if there are specific people you want to have at the meeting. For example: I would like the school psychologist or a district behavior specialist to attend the meeting.]*

*I can meet on: _____ [Add dates/times].*

*I look forward to your response.*

*Sincerely,*

*(Signature)*

## CHAPTER 13
# BIP

A Behavior Intervention Plan (BIP), will follow the FBA. The BIP provides appropriate support, tools, and skills to the child and the school staff so that challenging behaviors are reduced. The goals of the BIP should be positive behaviors that the student can learn and that will replace those negative ones.

Positive behaviors need positive support. Positive supports in a BIP can include the following:

- *Changing something in the environment to take away the triggers of the behavior.*
- *Changing how adults respond to the behavior.*
- *Educating the student about the triggers for the behavior*
- *Providing the student with appropriate social skills instruction*
- *Providing the student with counseling services to help him identify and manage the emotions that trigger the behavior.*

The BIP should include rewards for replacing negative behaviors with positive ones. It is important to include the student in selecting rewards, so they are actually motivating the student. Rewards might be an extra break or a few minutes of playground time, 10 minutes shooting basketball, computer time, eating lunch with a preferred staff member or other individual attention from an adult, or a positive note home.

The BIP should also include a system for tracking the student's behavior and for determining whether the BIP is successful. The IEP Team might use emails to parents, behavior charts, or sticker sheets to collect data on any improvements in the targeted behaviors. Remember that the BIP is part of the student's IEP. It must be followed by the school staff, and it should be reviewed and changed as needed and as required by law.

In some instances, an FBA may be prompted by an event leading to a change in the student's placement, requiring the school to complete the assessment within ten days. Children without a current 504 or IEP can still qualify for a BIP; however, if a BIP is deemed necessary, additional support is likely needed.

Understanding the behaviors exhibited by your child is crucial in determining appropriate resolutions. If you're seeking ideas or guidance, an IEP Advocate can be invaluable in such situations. Advocates excel in creating plans and offering realistic resolutions within the school's framework.

While advocates can be beneficial, they are not mandatory. The school is there to support you, and if they fall short, you have the right to file a complaint. It's important to recognize and exercise your rights to ensure your child receives the necessary support and interventions.

# CHAPTER 14
# OCR

OCR stands for the Office of Civil Rights, a subagency of the US Department of Education. The primary goal is to enforce the numerous federal civil rights laws that prohibit discrimination in programs or activities that receive federal assistance from the Department of Education. This includes addressing issues related to discrimination based on race, color, national origin, sex, disability, and age. The OCR investigates complaints filed by individuals who believe their rights have been violated and also conducts proactive compliance reviews to ensure educational institutions are upholding the principles of nondiscrimination. The OCR will enforce the following:

- *Title VI of the Civil Rights Act of 1964, prohibits discrimination on the basis of race, color, or national origin.*

- *Title IX of the Education Amendments of 1972, prohibits discrimination on the basis of sex.*

- *Section 504 of the Rehabilitation Act of 1973, prohibits discrimination on the basis of disability.*

- *The Age Discrimination Act of 1975, prohibits discrimination on the basis of age.*

- *Title II of the Americans with Disabilities Act of 1990, prohibits discrimination on the basis of disability.*

- *Boy Scouts of America Equal Access Act, which prohibits denial of access to or other discrimination against the Boy Scouts or other Title 36 U.S.C. youth groups in public elementary schools, public secondary schools, local education agencies, and state education agencies that have a designated open forum or limited public forum.*

It is crucial to recognize that public schools and public charter schools are influenced by two distinct entities. Different organizations will conduct their own investigations, with the Office for Civil Rights (OCR) generally not delving deeply into the Individualized Education Program (IEP) process, as it is typically managed by the state. This holds true at least in North Carolina.

However, the OCR will scrutinize the state if there are indications that it is not adhering to its policies regarding the IEP process. We have submitted four OCR complaints. Yes, four. It's important to note that this process takes time; it is not a swift turnaround for results. State complaints typically conclude within 30 to 45 days, though the OCR does not explicitly outline a timeline for their investigations. As of now, the outcomes of these filings are still pending and in progress.

We consulted with our attorney to dissect the extensive list of wrongdoings, and he skillfully categorized them for us into various actionable groups for proper filing. When faced with any form of wrongdoing, and the decision to file a formal complaint emerges as the most suitable course of action, it is advisable to engage in a structured note-taking process.

Sit down and meticulously jot down the aspects that evoke your concern. Document the elements that serve as evidence and provide context that fortifies your argument. Take the time to repeat this exercise on several occasions, allowing yourself the freedom to utilize as many pages as necessary. Remember, this process is for your benefit, aiding in the clarity and strength of your case.

Drawing from personal experience, when emotions are heightened, and feelings are exposed things can often blur together. In my case, intense anger initially clouded my perception of individual issues, only later realizing that they were indicative of broader wrongdoing. For instance, the act of making my son sit at the quiet table as a punishment due to his inability to control his tics, despite prior communication with the school, exemplified discrimination. Similarly, holding the school accountable for punishing him in response to his expression of suicidal ideations constituted retaliation.

In crafting your complaint, don't shy away from using precise and impactful terms. These words serve as your classifications for the wrongdoings you're addressing. While providing examples is crucial, keep them succinct on the complaint forms. I strongly recommend maintaining a comprehensive file containing all your supporting evidence—email communications, and any other relevant proof. This organized documentation will be invaluable in substantiating your case.

You don't necessarily need an attorney to file a complaint; the process is surprisingly straightforward, despite initial feelings of being overwhelmed. To access the complaint form, a simple Google search for "OCR Department of Education complaint" will suffice. Once found, you can easily print the PDF, fill it out online, and either submit it electronically or complete the digital copy and submit that.

It's worth noting that the consent form might seem a bit cumbersome as it requires a wet signature. You have a 20-day window after submission to complete this form. In our case, we used a mobile app that transforms photos into scanned documents. This allowed us to convert the image to a PDF and directly email it to the OCR; you'll find the email address on the complaint form.

It's important to note that you don't need to submit the "proof" right away. The OCR will initiate contact with you, review the complaint, and determine if it warrants an investigation. Once assigned, you'll receive a case number that will accompany you throughout the process. The electronic version allows for a more detailed description than the PDF.

Complaints are accepted by the OCR within 180 days of the time of the alleged incident. If this timeline is exceeded, the OCR provides a waiver for explaining the delay, and they will assess whether the reason is valid for an extension.

Upon receiving the consent form and complaint, the OCR may reach out for further clarification or supporting documentation if necessary. This step ensures that the process is thorough and comprehensive.

Sometimes the OCR will dismiss a complaint. The OCR does not have the authority to investigate complaints for reason that include:

- *The complaint fails to state a violation of one of the laws OCR enforces.*
- *The complaint was not filed in a timely manner (within 180 calendar days of the date of the alleged*

*discrimination) and a waiver of the timeliness requirement was not granted.*

- *The allegations raised by the complaint have been resolved and are therefore no longer appropriate for investigation.*

- *A signed consent form is required to proceed with an investigation and the consent form has not been provided within 20 days of requesting the signed form.*

The OCR has its methods of discovery and will seek and receive information from both parties. You will be able to discuss the matters at hand with the investigator, they will most likely set a time to review the timeline and complaint you filed in detail.

It's worth noting that on the complaint form, there's an option to check a box indicating your agreement to "mediation" if the school is willing to participate. Schools often opt for mediation because, while the OCR primarily enforces systemic changes and seldom results in financial resolutions, these complaints can significantly impact the school's reputation. Furthermore, once filed, the complaints become public information.

The OCR is diligent in monitoring and ensuring that the school complies with necessary changes. As you embark on this process, it's crucial to reflect on your desired outcomes. What do you hope to achieve, and what are your anticipated results? Understanding your goals will guide your approach throughout the complaint resolution process.

Let's consider a hypothetical scenario where you've chosen mediation on your complaint, and the school has agreed. A date will be scheduled for the mediation process, and the OCR mediators will contact you to discuss the logistics and outline what the day will entail. Typically, these mediations are conducted virtually, given that the OCR office is located in DC. They'll advise you to set aside 4-7 hours for the mediation.

On the designated day, the school will have their attorney present, and if you have an attorney, they can also be on the call. However, it's important to note that having an attorney is not a necessity, and foregoing one can save you money. The OCR mediators are skilled at maintaining the meeting's focus.

When the mediation begins, all parties will enter the virtual room together to review the rules and expectations. It's up to you how much you want to express during the process. It's worth noting that the school may not initiate the conversation, so be prepared to guide the discussion based on your concerns and desired outcomes.

It's important to understand that the mediators are not there to assign blame or establish guilt. This means there's no need to come prepared to defend your case as this is not a hearing or trial. Your preparation should involve creating a simple statement explaining why you are participating in the mediation, and this will be expected during the process.

Moreover, you are not obligated to stay in the same virtual room as the school representatives. If preferred, you can request to be separated into private rooms. The mediators will facilitate this setup, and all you need is a clear connection and a webcam. Once in your designated room, the mediator will inquire about your specific requests or "asks." They will ensure a clear understanding before presenting your perspective to the school representatives in the other room.

Asks can vary widely; consider creative options. For instance, request staff training by a third-party IEP specialist, sessions for parents to understand the EC process, handbook amendments reflecting OCR's contact information, a clear mental health crisis plan for students and families, and potential asks for private school funding, therapy, or costs to offset wrongdoing. Let your imagination guide your requests to address specific incidents and contribute positively to the educational environment.

If you have a specific amount in mind, be prepared with that figure. It's often prudent to split your request into "monetary" and "non-monetary" categories. While it's exceptionally rare for school boards to terminate employees despite allegations, particularly in charter schools, requesting the removal of someone from their position might be deemed unrealistic by the OCR. However, in my opinion, it's worth going for it.

After the mediator leaves, be prepared for a potential wait—this could be as short as 20 minutes or extend to hours. Unfortunately, a prolonged waiting period doesn't necessarily indicate positive outcomes, as frustrating as that may be.

It's crucial to note that mediations are considered "confidential." Before engaging in the process, you'll sign a confidentiality agreement with the OCR, prohibiting discussion of the meeting with anyone. Importantly, anything that transpires in mediation cannot be applied to the case or investigation if you decide to walk away, and the case reverts to the OCR. Even if the school admits fault or denies allegations during mediation, no consequences may ensue. Mediators are also bound by confidentiality and cannot disclose the discussions or findings to investigators.

If you find yourself in mediation and the school is not meeting you even a fraction of the way, you have every right to walk away. Actually, at any time you can walk for any reason. For example, if you request a few years of tuition and the school counters with two thousand dollars, or if they ask you to revoke pending complaints and sign away your rights to further litigation without addressing your concerns adequately, walking away is a valid option. It's important to know that if you choose to leave, the case goes back to the OCR for investigation.

Following your decision to leave mediation, a closure letter will come from the OCR, officially closing the case, and assigning a new case number to an investigator who will commence the actual investigation. This investigation process can span from three months to a year, and unfortunately, specific timelines are not provided.

If you reach an agreement during mediation, the complaint essentially disappears as if it never happened. This is often why schools opt for mediation—it allows for resolution without a lasting mark against them. While the OCR will respond if the school fails to uphold its end of the deal, the original complaint itself will vanish, and no official record will be held against the school.

It's worth noting that the OCR operates throughout the entire country and has hundreds, if not thousands of cases to deal with. While their processes may take a considerable amount of time, there's a sense that they might be more thorough than their state-level counterparts.

It's completely understandable to feel nervous when dealing with a large organization like the OCR, but the process is surprisingly straightforward. The OCR attorneys who reach out are also very accessible and have been able to answer all my questions thoroughly. The most challenging aspect is the waiting period; things rarely move as quickly as we would like, especially when it involves our children. Patience is key during this process.

# CHAPTER 15
# A BREAK

Intrusive thoughts, by nature, are transient, and not meant to persist indefinitely. However, a lingering question arises: when does an intrusive thought transform into a persistent mindset? The ongoing internal emotional conflict instigated by this charter school continues to unfold, leaving me uncertain about the prospect of ever recognizing a metaphorical white flag.

As I navigate the maze of thoughts and emotions, attempting to reconcile their ebb and flow, the aftermath of challenging the school and those involved still echoes within me. Every conceivable system designed to aid individuals in such situations became my battlefield. The investment of countless hours in this pursuit of whatever this is was necessary.

In the midst of all of this, the idea of collecting my experiences in a book took root. The envisioned manuscript aimed to fill its pages not only with my own validation but also with guidance for others grappling with similar challenges. Reflecting on the journey, I can't help but ponder if possessing half the knowledge I now have would have altered the outcome. Perhaps a different path would have emerged, steering the narrative in a direction not initially foreseen.

Truth be told it has been weeks since I have written a word because I don't know what to say. I thought putting into words the reality of what actually happened, my son's story would be harder than talking about how to navigate through the processes; I was wrong. I am having a hard time swallowing that pill. The book was supposed to be a guide, not a road to a wall. I don't have the answers. I wanted nothing more than to say that our systems prevailed, however, that is not the case.

So, I took a break.

The cloud of all these thoughts has overwhelmed my mind, and the sense of hopelessness has become more than just intrusive; it's shaping my overall outlook. I hesitate to label the system as entirely broken, and I believe people do care. I want to assist you in not experiencing the same despair I feel. Will my words serve as inspiration for you to fight, or will my book only confirm the bleak notion that there's no hope, and our education system is irreparably damaged?

I've grappled with the reality in which I find myself. Lost in thought, I'd stand at the sink, brushing my teeth until there was no toothpaste left. I found myself contemplating discarding this entire idea and accepting the loss. My son is now attending a new school, slowly recovering from the trauma. We could walk away from all of this. Fortunately, I'm blessed with a team of educators who genuinely care, and I witness every day how misguided that charter school was. Since we left, my feelings have been validated more than once. I've concluded that I can't remain silent; validation is profoundly meaningful, and I know there are others out there who share similar experiences.

Losing sight of a goal can be daunting at times, but it doesn't equate to defeat. It presents an opportunity for reassessment and application. While I aspired to possess all the answers, my primary objective was to convey to others that they were not alone. I genuinely believe in the power of knowledge, and the more individuals who are informed, the better. Raising awareness was the initial goal; sharing a story to inspire others might yield diverse results for someone else. Don't you think? This story is my pebble, and while it may not change the world, it will undoubtedly create ripples. I have to consistently remind myself of that.

As we move forward, I may not provide you with all of the answers, but I can offer validation. I am revitalized and prepared to persist in whatever this journey entails.

# CHAPTER 16
# NCDPI

The North Carolina Department of Public Instruction, commonly known as the NCDPI or simply the DPI for those in North Carolina, plays a crucial role in the state's education system. Referred to as "the state" in the context of this discussion, it is noteworthy that the state's complaint resolution process is currently facing significant challenges.

On the official state website, the NCDPI declares its commitment to providing leadership and services in various essential areas, including curriculum and instruction, accountability, finance, teacher and administrator preparation and licensing, professional development, and school business support and operations.

The State exercises its influence and support over 115 local public school districts, 2,500+ district public schools, 200+ charter schools, and three residential schools dedicated to students with hearing and visual impairments.

The hierarchy within the NCDPI follows a stringent chain of command, with Catherine Truitt holding the top position as the State Superintendent. This position, an elected one, was assumed by Truitt in January 2021. Accompanying her is Dr. Carol Ann Hudgens, who joined the NCDPI in April 2023 as the Senior Director of EC.

Dr. Hudgens expressed her enthusiasm about her recent appointment, stating, "I look forward to embracing this new leadership role, as it affords me the opportunity to persist in advocating for children with disabilities, their families, local leaders of EC programs, and the exceptional children teachers and service providers throughout the state. I am committed to supporting the dedicated staff within the NCDPI Office of Exceptional Children."

In the coming days, Dr. Hudgens emphasized the importance of reviewing current successes and strategically prioritizing areas where collective efforts can yield the greatest impact. As plans for the upcoming school year take shape, she aims to ensure that their collective efforts align with the goal of enhancing the educational experience for the students of North Carolina. Dr. Hudgens expressed gratitude for the ongoing work and the continued commitment to the students of the state.

When it comes to IEPs, the state assumes responsibility for addressing concerns. If your school fails to honor an IEP request or deviates from the specifications of an existing IEP, reaching out to the state becomes a necessary step.

However, it's important to note that the DPI has limitations in its jurisdiction. The DPI exclusively handles IEP-related matters and does not intervene in cases involving 504 plans, discrimination, retaliation, or harassment, regardless of the circumstances, those cases will need to be funneled through the OCR. This presents a complex situation for parents, as these issues are often interconnected, making it challenging to address them separately.

The clear demarcation of responsibilities between the state and the DPI underscores the need for a comprehensive approach to handling educational concerns. Parents may find themselves navigating multiple channels to address various aspects of their child's educational experience, highlighting the importance of a holistic and collaborative approach within the educational system.

# CHAPTER 17
# THE PROCESS

The complaint process is streamlined and user-friendly, the fillable complaint form is readily accessible on the DPI's website or through a Google search. This form can be submitted via email, fax, or traditional mail directly to the DPI. Unlike the OCR process, there is no requirement for a wet signature for consent.

When submitting the complaint, it is crucial to also send a copy to the Superintendent of the Local Education Agency (LEA) or the Head of School of the charter school where the child is enrolled. Simultaneous notification ensures that relevant local authorities are informed of the complaint. Importantly, there is no need to attach any supporting documents to the copy you send the school, in fact, I would advise against it. Instead, it is recommended to keep the form concise and attach a separate page providing detailed facts and supporting evidence, on the copy you send to the DPI. This approach helps maintain clarity and facilitates a focused review of the presented concerns.

I can't say I was ever comfortable with the school, seeing that you had filed a complaint against them. I think this opens up opportunities for further harassment and retaliation, neither of which the DPI will follow up on. The complaint usually takes 30-45 days to process and that is a long time to go with an upset administrator, and a child already having struggles. In our charter school, the principal and the superintendent held grudges and made things way worse for us. Though it is hard to determine if the retaliation and increased harassment were a result of a DPI complaint or the fact, that I challenged them; we will never know.

In the first section, you will complete the basic complainant information, student information, and public agency information. In section two you will disclose the alleged violations by the date on which they occurred and provide supporting facts. Remember to keep it brief, usually just the violation itself. Don't give the school an opportunity to build their case against you, they will see it first. Write as much as you need to on the attached document.

As I said I would write in that box that there is an attachment with supporting facts, this is solely because this document has to go back to the school, and they will be able to view it before the state will start working on it.

The complaint must allege a violation that occurred not more than one year prior to the date that the complaint was received. Once you submit the complaint, a few days to a week later you should receive an encrypted email providing you with a complaint number, and an outline of the allegations. The letter will be addressed to you and the school. There will be an opportunity for the school to submit their documents to defend their stance. They will usually have their attorneys complete this. They will be given usually 15 days from the date of the encrypted email to provide the requested documentation. You will also be assigned an investigator or a Dispute Resolution Specialist.

Now you wait. Once the DPI completes its investigation, it will send another encrypted email with either an "in-compliance or non-compliant" letter and a report.

It is crucial to understand that the DPI does not entertain appeals. They do not seek clarification on subjective matters, nor do they conduct a second-look process through internal reviews. The DPI remains steadfast in not overturning decisions, even if the school's response is proven false.

Welcome to the North Carolina Department of Public Instruction.

In the rare event that the state finds a school to be non-compliant, it will be subject to resolution. The complaint form you submitted includes a section for your proposed resolution. Essentially, the school will receive a mark against them, and they will be required to outline corrective measures to prevent a recurrence. However, there are no financial penalties, monitoring, removal from positions, or even an obligation to issue an apology.

## CHAPTER 18
# OUR 1ST DPI EXPERIENCE

Our charter school exhibited no remorse whatsoever. From their perspective, they believed they hadn't erred, and it was my mistake to demand that my child receive an equal educational opportunity. I dedicated considerable effort to understanding how to file these complaints, meticulously gathering all required documents. I even sought the guidance of an attorney to navigate me through the process.

My initial complaint revolved around the school's failure to initiate an IEP assessment, a request I made in writing via email. However, the school's response threw me off track. They asked if I wanted to remove the existing 504 plan, which derailed my efforts. It was at this juncture that they protected themselves. Unfamiliar with the intricacies of these processes, I hesitated and responded, "No, let's keep the 504 in place." The truth was, I had put in tremendous effort to secure this inadequate 504 plan, one that they barely adhered to in the first place.

I found myself reaching for any term or concept I'd heard of—FBA, BIPs—hoping one might resonate. Feeling overwhelmed, I reached out to an IEP advocate from Raleigh. We discussed the situation in detail, and the most critical point was realizing that I could request an IEP while the 504 plan remained in place.

In response, I emailed the school, informing them of my conversation with the IEP advocate and correcting their misinformation. The counselor had stopped responding, and it was the school principal who replied, asserting that the counselor had intended to convey that an assessment could proceed while retaining the 504 plans. However, this still didn't trigger the assessment process. The principal added that they had personally observed my son in class for 45 minutes and noted his apparent disengagement. They suggested that the upcoming 504 meeting would provide an opportunity to discuss why my child seemed disinterested in the classroom work. Additionally, the principal hinted at the 504 meeting as a platform to address the IEP process.

At that moment, I was utterly appalled. The response left me speechless—I didn't know how to react. It became apparent that an IEP assessment wasn't going to happen; the EC team wasn't even involved. The scheduled meeting passed without any mention of an IEP. Throughout the year, it felt as though my son was clinging to a rope tied to a speeding car. He held on desperately while the driver, oblivious and uncaring, showed no intention of slowing down. Ultimately, this neglectful approach led my son to a point where he contemplated giving up entirely and didn't want to live.

I made sure to include the emails as supporting evidence in a very explicit statement submitted to the DPI with my complaint. I waited anxiously for a response. When I finally received an encrypted email, the initial letter indicated that the school was deemed non-compliant. However, just five hours later, another letter arrived from the DPI stating the opposite—that the school had indeed complied. This contradiction left me bewildered. I reached out via email, and she apologized, confirming that the second letter was accurate; the school had allegedly fulfilled its obligations. It left me uncertain about what steps to take next.

I drafted a comprehensive and lengthy email to Dr. Hudgens, expressing my deep disappointment in her perceived failure and urging her to recognize the gravity of these complaints. I emphasized that parents don't resort to filing complaints with the DPI on a whim. It's a measure of desperation after exhausting all other avenues. I emphasized that DPI represents our final hope for resolution, yet it seemed Dr. Hudgens wasn't dedicating the necessary time to grasp the essence of these complaints. As parents, we're left in the dark about the precise language or strategy needed to make our grievances impactful.

Regrettably, I never received a direct response from Dr. Hudgens. However, I did receive an email from a DPI compliance officer, presumably at Dr. Hudgens' request. We had a detailed call, meticulously discussing the complaint. I felt there might be something crucial missing from my understanding. Although she couldn't divulge the specifics of what the school submitted, she informed me that I could request that documentation. It became crucial for me to review what they had presented. I needed to ensure I hadn't overlooked any critical information, albeit I doubted there was much I missed.

I utilized the NCDPI's "Public Request Form" to obtain documentation related to the specific complaint filed through the DPI. Upon receiving the materials, the school submitted to defend their case, it was evident that their attorney's letter presented "facts" that were largely untrue or subjective. I immediately delved into debunking each assertion made by the attorney. For every claimed falsehood, I provided substantial evidence and offered contextual clarification for the subjective statements.

Upon sending my comprehensive report back to the DPI, I was informed that the absence of an appeals process rendered the situation challenging. However, I had a conversation with the Dispute Resolution Consultant for the state. She acknowledged that based on the information provided, there was a possibility of interpreting the case in my favor. However, she asked, "What good would it do if they were found non-compliant?" This caught me off guard. Despite my son no longer attending that school, I insisted that their behavior was unjust and should be addressed.

When I emphasized that my concerns extended beyond just my son and that the school's behavior was fundamentally wrong, she expressed an unfortunate reality: despite recognizing where the school erred, there seemed to be no course of action available to rectify the situation.

The weight of hopelessness bore down on me after I hung up; anger surged within. I searched for someone to hold accountable. Seeking answers, I reached out again, questioning further. The first complaint had been dismissed, leading to nothing substantial. In essence, the school had emerged victorious.

Resignation isn't part of my nature. I felt compelled to explore every avenue to grasp the extent of this flawed system if there was any hope of mending it. Reaching out to the DPI once more, I arranged a call with a Section Chief for the Policy, Monitoring, and Audit Office of Exceptional Children.

During this call, I was introduced to the concept of "child find" and encouraged to file a new complaint with the DPI. Understanding that filing the same complaint would result in immediate dismissal, I realized I had to take a different approach. This revelation infused me with a glimmer of optimism, providing a small reserve of strength to revisit and meticulously sift through the mountains of communications, preparing to construct yet another complaint.

# CHAPTER 19
# CHILD FIND

Under federal law, a paramount responsibility of public schools is to actively seek, identify, and assess children who may require special education services. This imperative mandate encompasses youngsters from birth to the age of 21, ensuring a comprehensive reach throughout the educational spectrum. Notably, the scope of this legislation extends beyond the traditional school setting, encompassing homeschooled and privately educated children, as well as those who are migrants or without stable homes. The inclusivity of this federal law is further underscored by its application across every state in the United States, subject to scrutiny by both state authorities and the Office for Civil Rights (OCR).

This federal law, rooted in the Individuals with Disabilities Education Act (IDEA), recognizes that the proactive identification of children in need is a crucial initial step toward providing them with the necessary support to thrive academically. When a school becomes aware of or suspects that a child may have a disability, it is incumbent upon the educational institution to conduct a comprehensive evaluation of the child's needs. This process, known as Child Find, is an integral component of the broader legislative framework designed to address the unique educational requirements of children with disabilities.

The overarching purpose of IDEA is to ensure that children with disabilities receive an education tailored to their individual needs. In pursuit of this objective, each state, in collaboration with its public schools, is mandated to formulate and implement policies and procedures for the effective identification of children who may benefit from special education services. Moreover, practical methods must be developed to discern which children qualify for specialized education and related support services, thereby facilitating a tailored and inclusive approach to their academic development. This commitment to comprehensive support underscores the nation's dedication to fostering an educational environment where every child, regardless of their unique needs, has the opportunity to thrive and succeed.

This sounds great, the school actually manages their student's education despite the various challenges they might face. Yeah, right. Our charter school and many others will continue to fall negligent of this expectation. They will place the responsibility back on the parents and will neglect to inform them of the federal laws that are designed to help children.

Child Find initiatives are designed to identify and address a diverse range of challenges that children and youth may face, warranting a comprehensive assessment. Various factors may trigger the need for evaluation under Child Find, including diagnosed or suspected intellectual, physical, or emotional disabilities that hinder a child's ability to derive full benefit from a standard school program without specialized assistance. My recent conversation with the Department of Public Instruction (DPI) highlighted that indicators of such challenges may manifest in academic performance, behavioral patterns, mental health struggles, and deviations from typical social skills.

In light of these concerns, it becomes imperative for schools to be vigilant and responsive to the needs of their students. When issues or struggles emerge, whether evident in grades, behavioral dynamics, mental health challenges, or deviations from expected social norms, the educational institution is obligated to take note. In response to these observations, the school should proactively initiate a formal request for a comprehensive evaluation, mirroring the process associated with an Individualized Education Program (IEP) request.

Upon submitting the assessment request, the school is then required to promptly notify parents of their intention to conduct an evaluation and provide explicit reasons for doing so. This communication is crucial for maintaining transparency and fostering collaboration between educators and parents in addressing the unique needs of the child. Subsequently, a mutually agreeable date is determined to conduct the assessment, ensuring that the process is thorough and considerate of the child's individual circumstances.

Following the assessment, a meeting is convened to discuss the findings. This collaborative gathering involves parents, educators, and relevant specialists to collectively analyze the evaluation results and determine the most appropriate course of action. This holistic approach, rooted in open communication and shared decision-making, reflects the commitment of educational institutions to address the diverse needs of every student and ensure that they receive the specialized support required for academic success and personal development.

## CHAPTER 20
# OUR 2$^{ND}$ DPI COMPLAINT

After persistently seeking clarification and striving to comprehend why the initial complaint wasn't resolved in our favor, I took the opportunity to engage with someone at the DPI (Department of Public Instruction). They provided recommendations and explanations that led me to pursue a second complaint, emphasizing the significance of the 'child find' statute.

Feeling a renewed sense of hope in the DPI's concern, I diligently assembled an airtight case supported by images and comprehensive documentation to reinforce my assertions. I did all that I could on my part and even consulted with the DPI representative who reassured me that my case would be thoroughly reviewed, emphasizing their commitment to ensuring a fair and just resolution. The individual I had been corresponding with even suggested directing the complaint specifically to her, rather than the general email address I had previously used. It was an emotional roller coaster.

Following the guidance given, I submitted the complaint as instructed, also forwarding a copy to the superintendent as required. I prepared myself to wait, feeling confident and ready to inform my son that appropriate action had been taken regarding the unacceptable behavior. I was prepared for the system to ensure justice prevailed. I received my letter of acknowledgment and the information they were requesting from the school, I had seen these letters before, so I glanced at it and didn't really read it. A couple of days after it came through, I went back to reference something in particular and I realized it was not my complaint.

It turned out that the complaint was meant for an entirely different school, belonging to someone else. That sinking feeling returned as if history was about to repeat itself, and my confidence in the system began to wane. Despite reaching out and highlighting their mistake, they hadn't yet recognized it. Eventually, they resent the correct letter, but now I faced a deadline for the accurate case and school.

I marked the deadline on my calendar, striving to maintain a positive outlook. On the appointed day, I received an encrypted email containing the report and the letter. Once again, to my dismay, the DPI had sided with the school – somehow finding them compliant, It left me bewildered: how could this be?

Deep down, despite my efforts to stay positive, a nagging feeling persisted, hinting at this inevitable outcome. The school seemed to have influential ties within the DPI. In fact, the mom who managed the school's Facebook group, the same person who removed and blocked me, worked for the NCDPI. I began to question my own naivety in believing that this process would yield fair results.

Inevitably, I found myself in a despondent state. I penned yet another letter to Dr. Hudgens, but it remained unanswered. Feeling compelled, I followed up a few days later, expressing regret if my earlier communication had been too direct. I requested her time to discuss the process, hoping for a clearer understanding, yet even this attempt went unanswered.

It became painfully evident that Dr. Hudgens had no intention of engaging with me or any other concerned parent seeking a resolution. What was her purpose? Her actions contradicted the mission statement she represented, displaying a lack of concern or empathy for our plight.

I submitted the public document request through the DPI, and I received the documents back, much like the first time. I was even more sick when I got this set of documents back. The school's attorney sent their rebuttal, much like the first time. The response started very casually by addressing the investigator by her first name. I share this because this is what parents will be up against and this is what the DPI will allow as an appropriate and convincing response from the school.

*"As you know I am helping \*\*\* with the various complaints filed against it by \*\*\*\*. She has now filed four DPI complaints against \*\*\* in the last few months. DPI rejected two, found for \*\*\* in one, and this is currently the last open \*\*\* complaint."*

*"You need to know that Mrs. \*\*\* "problems" with \*\*\* did not surface until she was banned initially from entering the school in December 2022, and subsequently from the carpool line, too, in May 2023 because of multiple instances of inappropriate conduct toward staff members including shouting, profane language and inappropriate gestures involving her middle finger. Since then, she has engaged in a vendetta against \*\*\* and it's staff". – Schools Attorney's Defense to NCDPI*

I read further as the attorney narrated an image of me that could not have been more untrue and mixed blatant lies into his defense. I always wondered how attorneys represent those who are truly wrong or guilty, I guess they just lie.

*"Agreeing to provide frequent communication in a standardized format does not suggest a need for special education services. In this situation, \*\*\* agreed to it in a good-faith attempt to be transparent with \*\*\*'s parents so they might calm down. We are providing an example of the communication sheet, which the \*\*\*'s designed and asked be used."* – Schools Attorney's defense to NCPDI

The attorney continued to present a defense that egregiously violated the procedures outlined in the Individuals with Disabilities Education Improvement Act (IDEIA), specifically concerning discrimination within the realm of special education. One of the most appalling moments came when he made a statement so profound it seemed to send shivers through the very core of existence, words that could make God himself shake his head.

He callously argued that because our son had only expressed a single instance of self-harm as a threat, it should not be considered a credible one. His words felt like a twist of the knife, a stark disregard for the gravity of mental health concerns and the intricate complexities of a child's distress. It was as though the attorney's words carried an eerie weight as if even the divine might have shuddered at such callous reasoning.

This assertion not only overlooked the severity of the situation but also failed to acknowledge the critical importance of addressing any hint of self-harm or mental health distress with utmost concern and care. The chilling casualness with which the attorney downplayed our son's cry for help was not only legally objectionable but also morally disturbing.

I find myself accepting criticism, even when it's harsh or laced with words like 'vendetta.' I've developed a thick skin over time, understanding that opinions can vary widely. However, what I cannot reconcile is the notion that a single instance of my son expressing thoughts of self-harm wasn't taken seriously simply because it was expressed only once. This is a stark reminder of the alarming inadequacies in our school systems' approaches to mental health.

The responsibility that the US Supreme Court leaves to the schools, particularly concerning 'how' they address such critical issues, is immense. Yet, what we often witness is glaring deficiencies in their response to mental health crises. The dismissal or underestimation of a cry for help, even if it's just once, is a disheartening reflection of the flawed system in place to safeguard our children within educational environments.

I also attempted to connect with Catherine Truitt, reaching out through numerous calls and emails, urging for a meeting to discuss the challenges not only I but many others were facing within the realm of EC (Exceptional Children) support. Unfortunately, Truitt's response was nonexistent, which, to be honest, wasn't surprising. It felt as though unless there was a staged photo opportunity, she wouldn't bother showing up.

The absence of any appeals meant that even if the school were to come forward and confess, admitting fault, it wouldn't sway their decision. The process had reached its endpoint, and I found myself hitting a wall, the one that the road in North Carolina leads to.

It's become apparent that I possess an inherent inability to simply let things be. This sentiment echoes loudly in my actions thus far. Driven by the conviction to navigate the system as intended, I opted to exercise my rights as a parent. With resolve, I committed to traversing the hierarchical ladder once more.

Repeatedly, I reached out through emails and phone calls, directing my efforts towards what I labeled as "the team" – a group of women who seemed to oversee the North Carolina Department of Public Instruction akin to a casual book club. There appeared to be a lack of substantial accountability, merely convening to discuss their readings and learnings before moving on. In my mind's eye, I sketched out this entire scenario, allowing my research to unravel the interconnectedness between these individuals.

After what seemed like a borderline case of harassment on my part for a couple of weeks, an unexpected email from Dr. Carol Ann Hudgens herself landed in my inbox. The acknowledgment of all my attempts to communicate was startling. She graciously invited me to send my queries, assuring me of her willingness to address them. The rush of adrenaline was palpable as I hastily concluded my grocery run, powering through my nightly routine to compose a meticulously detailed list of questions.

Referencing the complaint lodged and the attorney's arguments against the inaccuracies, I probed deeply into their perspectives on matters pertaining to IDEA (Individuals with Disabilities Education Act) and FAPE

(Free Appropriate Public Education). The effort invested in this correspondence was immense. As I hit 'send', a surge of confidence washed over me. This was it – an unassailable argument that would compel them to acknowledge their errors and rectify the situation.

Days turned into a week, and I adhered to what I deemed a "respectable" duration of waiting. Resuming my pursuit, I sent a singular email, inquiring if she required any clarification before responding. When her reply eventually arrived, it hit me like a familiar, yet crushing, brick. The realization struck me then that this response was something worth sharing, given Dr. Hudge's unwavering confidence led me to believe she wouldn't object to its dissemination.

*Hi, Ms. \*\*\*,*

*I received your inquiry today requesting a status on the responses to your questions. I have chosen to answer that email in this email where your questions were located.*

*Based on the series of questions you raised, most appear to be directly or indirectly related to the response to the complaint made by Mr. \*\*\* on behalf of his client. Additionally, many questions were expanded to seek my opinion or a basis for the opinions/statements of others.*

*The NCDPI does review the response provided by the school district; however, the facts in our final report are considered accurate if documented across multiple sources and in the documents requested in our intake letter. Both parties have the right to share their perspective of the dispute through the complaint itself and the response to the complaint. Our task is to determine the fact pattern across the multiple sources of information provided by both parties, meeting documentation, and the documents requested in the intake information.*

*Therefore, the NCDPI did not and does not weigh the written response of the district to the exclusion of details found across documents.*

**Carol Ann M. Hudgens, Ed.D. Senior Director**

*Office of Exceptional Children*

That was it.

NOPE, this was not going to be what I would accept.

*Carol,*

*Thank you for your previous response. I recognize the position my specific inquiries regarding my complaint may have placed you in. I would like to reformulate the questions in a more generalized manner for your consideration.*

*The intent behind my inquiry is to gain a clearer understanding of the role of the NCDPI in order to better support the educational process. As a state agency, the public has the right to seek information about the policies and procedures that impact our children's education outcomes.*

*Moving forward, please consider these questions in a general context without specific reference to my complaint.*

1. *When a parent submits a complaint to the DPI, is it mandatory to provide "supporting evidence" or*

*"additional documentation" to the school along with the complaint during the notification process? Is the state-developed complaint form sufficient notice that a complaint has been filed?*

2. *Regarding decision-making on complaints, you mentioned that the school and parents' statements are not the sole considerations. Could you elaborate on other factors that the NCDPI considers when determining the outcome of a complaint?*

3. *How does the NCDPI address false information provided by either party when there is no appeals process? What is the accuracy of the information verified, and what procedures are in place if false information is identified after the complaint's conclusion?*

4. *In NCDPI decisions, is there a reference or consideration of IDEA and FAPE? Why is verification of federal law not explicitly included in the conclusions of reports, or is it?*

5. *Does the NCDPI exclusively recognize external behaviors as grounds warranting special education services?*

6. *Are special education students required by the NCDPI to put forth equal effort in their Individualized Education Programs (IEPs)? Is meeting the school halfway a requirement for special education students?*

7. *Are references to prior cases permissible in the complaint process, or must current cases specifically relate to the matter at hand?*

8. Can you outline the requirements for obtaining a 504 and IEP? Is a diagnosis necessary for a 504? Is a diagnosis mandatory for an IEP?

9. Do privately obtained assessments by families outside of the school and the IEP assessment expire, making them irrelevant in pursuing an equal education?

10. Could you explain in your own words how the NCPDI perceives the stipulations of Child Find Sec 300.11?

11. Does an agreement such as "good faith" apply to all forms of special education services? If so, could you provide an outline of that section?

12. Considering deficiencies within this process, what steps are necessary to request an amendment or the implementation of new rules? How could an appeals process for all NCDPI complaints be established?

These questions address broader concerns about the general complaint process and the knowledge parents require when advocating for a child receiving special education services in North Carolina.

I eagerly anticipate your response.

Mrs ***

I already held the answers to most of these questions. It was evident that the broad scope of these inquiries was directly intertwined with my case. Yet, despite this clarity, my expectations of receiving a response from Dr. Hudgens dwindled. It was almost as though a response from her would inadvertently implicate not just herself but the entire North Carolina Department of Public Instruction (NCDPI) in their mishandling of cases like mine. So, perhaps her thought was to ignore it and maybe it would go away.

The involvement of Catherine Truitt in all the correspondence and her conspicuous silence in the face of the glaring issues didn't come as a shock. It was disappointing, albeit unsurprising. At this point, I had expected something like this would happen at the back of my mind, yet it still stung.

The crux of the matter lies in the exasperating realization that we are unable to establish a meaningful connection with these individuals – the very ones designated to assist us. Their unwillingness to lend an ear is confounding, leaving us wondering what steps to take next.

The truth, raw and undeniable, looms before us. It demands attention, making it impossible to turn a blind eye. Despite this, the deafening silence from those responsible for rectifying these matters persists. It's disheartening to witness the truth being blatantly ignored, forcing me once more to express my disappointment and disillusionment. Carol, it's evident - you've failed. The state has failed. There's an urgent call to do better, to mend the gaps, and to truly extend the support that is rightfully deserved.

## CHAPTER 21
## THE OTHERS...

Throughout this book, I've shared stories that aren't just mine; they're intertwined with the experiences of others. I felt compelled to include not only my own stories but also those that are heart-wrenching, frustrating, and, at times, infuriating. When I began this journey, I had no clear direction in mind. Yet, as I wrote, I found a newfound confidence, enabling me to guide others and share what they needed to hear.

In meeting other mothers, I realized they deserved their own space, a platform to express, "I hear you." I wish I could change everything for you, walk beside you into schools, and sit with you during meetings. If only I could use my "accosting" tone to draft the necessary emails for you, to ensure results. I understand the helplessness that engulfs you; I know the feeling when a school fails to recognize your child's worth, leaving you overwhelmed and disheartened.

You all inspired me to pursue certification as a board-certified IEP Advocate. It's officially on my to-do list. However, I chose to complete this book first because I believe certification isn't required to share my experiences and provide you with a roadmap that might lead to positive outcomes. I also need to clarify that mothers are not the only ones fighting for their kids, fathers, grandmothers, grandfathers, guardians, aunts, foster parents... anyone willing to fight for a child deserves this recognition.

**To the mom in the waiting room, you are not alone.**

While I was sitting in the waiting room at a psychologist's office, waiting on my son to complete some academic testing, so we can better align his IEP. There was a mom with her daughter. I had my laptop out and had every intention of working on this. However, that did not happen. The mother and daughter were trying really hard to complete the mountains of questions and were not having much success. It came as no surprise that she was having trouble focusing, considering where we were sitting. We were able to laugh and both of us tried to redirect her daughter. It was humorous because we were both so clearly comfortable with this type of behavior, it was second nature to us.

Someone came out and offered to help her daughter read through the questions in the other room. The Mom was able to breathe for a minute, and she was able to work on her own pile of questions needing to be completed. Once she finished, we got to talking. She told me more about her daughter and the challenges she was facing. While we were talking, I realized that both of us were facing similar difficulties. That is probably why we felt at ease with each other and were able to get on such friendly terms so quickly. I won't go into her daughter's details out of respect for both of them. I will say that the child was struggling, and it was rare for her to complete a class without intervention.

Her daughter attended a public Title I school in Charlotte. It had been almost 60 days since Mom had sent the school in writing an email, that in my opinion checked the required boxes for an IEP assessment. The school said that she needed to formally compose in writing an IEP request and has yet to actually acknowledge the request. I asked her to show me the email, and she did, and I was able to confirm, that while it did not use the "proper" terminology it did convey that an assessment was needed.

At this point, I'm no longer surprised by a school's negligence. I understand that Title I schools come with a reputation that is far from ideal; they often experience high teacher turnover rates. These schools have a greater need for accommodations, serving children who have been exposed to trauma or instability, factors that can impede the learning process. On top of these challenges, they also have students who are neurodivergent. It's safe to say that their already limited resources are stretched incredibly thin.

However, you will never hear me say that it's okay. I will never accept the excuse of 'that's Title I for you.' Children can't control where they live, the school they attend, or so much in their lives, yet they fall victim to a broken system every single day.

I guided her through the processes, being mindful not to overwhelm her with information. We discussed essential topics such as "child find", FBAs, and BIP. To ensure clarity, I made detailed notes on a sheet of paper and provided my cell phone number at the top, encouraging her to call or text if she ever felt lost or needed assistance. I know all too well the feeling of being overloaded with information and not even knowing where to start because, I too, was facing something very similar. She, like so many who are so limited in their options, doesn't have multiple choices; they have what they have, and they are expected to know how to navigate through it all.

## To the mom already filing her complaints... you are not alone

My child endured a terrible experience at school, where he was treated unfairly, and his right to an equal education was denied by an institution that seemed to lack an understanding of diversity. He reached a point where he would have preferred not to exist rather than continue feeling the way he did.

Reflecting on this experience and having conversations with other parents over the past year, I realize that I didn't fully appreciate the options available to me. I had the opportunity to pull him out and enroll him in a public school, luckily one with a high rating of 8/10. It struck me that our town, Huntersville, does not have any Title-1 schools, and yet I was initially distraught over the thought that he might miss out on opportunities.

During times of intense emotion and when faced with challenges, it's easy to lose sight of the fact that things could be worse. Many households don't even have the option to change schools. For those who do, it becomes a difficult decision, often choosing the lesser of two evils and hoping for the best.

None of which is in line with these directors' and superintendents' plans and agendas. They all promote equality acceptance, accountability ... all those words that should make us feel safe. They then are kept in a clear box, much like the pope because they know their actions and words don't align; and fear that someone might chuck their soda at them. They become untouchable.

I recently received a complaint from the DPI that turned out to be a mistake. It took me a day to realize this when I noticed that the names on the complaint were different. Astonishingly, the DPI had sent me another parent's complaint, and it had also been mistakenly sent to our charter school.

I promptly followed up with the DPI to bring this error to their attention. What adds another layer of concern is that this erroneous complaint was signed by Dr. Hudgens.

Being me, I took the time to read the entire complaint. It was passionately written and filled with intricate details. The mother had done an excellent job presenting the case. For a moment, I imagined myself as the investigator, trying to understand the situation with no prior context. However, I quickly stepped out of that perspective.

The depth of the complaint left me questioning how anyone could argue against it. While I acknowledge that schools have the right to present their side of the story, I couldn't fathom how this particular case could be disputed. I understand that some complaints may have room for resolution through various means, benefiting both parties involved, but in this instance, it seemed clear-cut.

This was a red button. I knew not to press the red button... but I did. I reached out to the mom, first in an email, which came off as incredibly creepy. So, I waited for what I thought to be the respective amount of time and then I called her. She was incredibly put off and wanted to know who I was and how I got her information. I was right to not make a joke, as it would have been taken poorly. I went on with who I was; I told her I was a mom in Mecklenburg

County who filed a complaint with the DPI as well. I explained that the DPI had sent me her information in error, because well – they were the DPI, and this was pretty par.

I admitted to the woman that curiosity had gotten the best of me, leading me to read her complaint. As we spoke over the phone, I could feel the depth of her emotions, which only served to validate my own feelings. She shared the various avenues she had pursued in an attempt to secure what was owed to her child. Sitting there, listening to her story, I couldn't help but feel a sense of helplessness on her behalf. In her pursuit of justice, all she had was a system that, unfortunately, appeared to be broken.

At the time of our conversation, she had not yet received a decision from the state, but I assured her that I would stay in touch. We delved into the unique struggles faced by moms of special needs children, emphasizing how our experiences often differ from those who can't relate. Life for us is a constant battle for basic rights, and inconveniences are a regular part of the journey.

As we shared stories, I couldn't help but feel a surge of anger—not because the situation was inherently wrong, as that was painfully clear, but because she lacked the options that I had. While I had the privilege of considering alternative schools, she was confined to a system that offered limited support.

She navigated through the complexities of the Individualized Education Program (IEP) with the help of state-funded programs providing advocacy services. Much like myself, she had become well-versed in the system through trial and error. Unfortunately, her child attended a

Title One school, leaving her without the option to simply pull him out and hope for the best.

Basic rights were being stripped away, and the already limited opportunities, hindered by systemic racism in our country, were further diminishing due to the school's negligence. All this was happening, and it felt like the state couldn't care less.

While kids are getting forgotten Catherine Truitt is creating plans for us. Plans that will aid in the overall well-being while rectifying the educational damages of the pandemic. I would challenge you to search IEP in that 44-page Polaris plan, you won't find it. In theory, these proposals are great, but if we continue to stack them on a shaky foundation and hide the realities in which we find ourselves they won't ever actually work.

I hung up with that mom, and again being me... not being able to leave well enough alone I wrote to Ms. Catherine Truitt. I might have to take a drive to Raliegh soon and get a better understanding of what she is priding herself on because I really just don't see it.

**To the mom at another charter school... you are not alone**

When the article surfaced and went viral in the small town of Huntersville (or Stepford, as it felt at times), a mother reached out to me. She explained that her daughter attended a charter school in the area, though not the same one as ours. At the time she conveyed her condolences for what had happened to our son and shared that her own daughter was facing some challenges.

I found myself pulled in multiple directions, metaphorically I was running around with a knife not sure who attacked first. I was like a small animal trapped against a wall with no place to run, no defense, and no protection. I tried to navigate the overwhelming emotions. Uncertain of how to process it all, I grappled with the awareness that something was deeply wrong, trapped in a constant cycle of negativity. At times, the turmoil within my own mind seemed more daunting than the reality around me.

I had heard from many parents who shared positive experiences, making me question if I was somehow mistaken or had done something wrong. I never argued with them. Instead, I expressed genuine happiness for their positive encounters and moved on. Therefore, I didn't want to create an issue where there wasn't one when this particular mom reached out. I distinctly recall feeling appreciative that she took the time to connect and show empathy.

It was halfway through the year when I received another message from her. She explained that things had taken a turn for the worse and expressed a genuine desire to talk. Without hesitation, I agreed. By that point, I had set aside the metaphorical knife and started writing about my experiences, putting me in a much better headspace.

We asked her to tell me all the things, I confirmed what I already knew and was given updates on her daughter since we last spoke. I asked her if I could share her story, and she said yes. Now, like the others, I will be keeping this pretty private so as not to open her up to any retaliation which we know these schools are capable of.

Her daughter was in the 5th grade and had been diagnosed with ADHD and anxiety, much like my son. Similar to him, she underwent testing when she was younger and was advised to retest. The complexity of autism spectrum disorder often overlaps with the ADHD spectrum, making it challenging to distinguish between the two. Although not everyone with ADHD experiences anxiety, it is a high likelihood for someone experiencing ADHD to have developed anxiety as well. this is probably because the ADHD can lead to challenges in cognitive functions, creating an environment where stress and anxiety may develop. It's not uncommon for doctors to recommend retesting for younger children.

She shared with me the difficulty in securing appointments with psychologists, with wait times extending up to 14 months. I provided her with names of places that might not be extensively covered by insurance but typically had sooner appointment availability. Despite the challenges, she was already receiving support from both a behavior specialist and a therapist.

Last year, she verbally requested an IEP assessment for her daughter, but the school insisted it wasn't necessary and opted to maintain the existing 504 plan. As the school year commenced, her daughter's grades began to decline. The child didn't respond well to being called out in front of the group, a daily occurrence that was noticeably affecting her demeanor. Her spark was fading, evident to her mother each day. In response, the mother began advocating more assertively for her daughter's needs.

This year, during a 504 meeting, the mom raised concerns about her daughter's challenges and the noticeable decline in grades. Interestingly, after these concerns were expressed, the grades seemingly improved—despite no actual changes in the situation. Funny how that works. How is this possible, you ask? Well, recall my earlier mention that charter schools create their own curriculum and grading systems. In this case, even though the 504 plan was supposed to provide necessary accommodations, the school had the flexibility to manipulate its grading system. Despite going over the accommodations the school had devised, which were barely being adhered to, the mom continued to express her belief that the current approach was ineffective.

I can only assume that this charter school had the same mentality that ours did, because who would make sure they didn't? Who actually cared if they acted unethically, the NCDPI didn't care that was apparent.

I guided her through the entire process, emphasizing the importance of documenting everything in writing. Given that she, like me, was neurodivergent, we decided that recording the interactions would be beneficial for her. I reminded her that North Carolina is a one-party consent state, meaning she didn't need to inform others of the recording.

My frustration surged when I discovered that she was told her 5th grader might not be cut out for college, as if such a determination could be made at such a young age. It was disheartening to hear such discouraging words from our educators—individuals who advocate for higher pay and more respect. The irony is almost comical, and regrettably, exceptional teachers are sometimes unfairly associated with the notion that teachers, in general, don't care.

She compiled a comprehensive list of everything she needed to do. During our two-and-a-half-hour conversation, my most significant takeaway was the overwhelming sense of failure she expressed. She admitted feeling frozen and uncertain about the next steps. It struck me that she believed she was failing simply because she didn't have all the answers. In reality, she was an exceptional mother, grappling with guilt and constraints beyond her control. Despite every feeling of inadequacy she harbored, I wanted to reassure her that meeting with a complete stranger to seek help for her daughter demonstrated her dedication and made her far from inadequate. She was, in fact, a great mother. Until challenged these schools seem like a great idea. The reality is that there is no support from the state and the schools know it, it's almost like it was by design. They will make you feel wrong, they will gaslight you and if you still manage to get up, they will run you out.

We delved into the core issue and discussed how it reached an impasse with the DPI. Her support went beyond mere validation; she empowered me to persist in this endeavor. The ever-expanding 'to-do' list became a topic of conversation. We explored the idea that if this expectation were shared among all parents, we could unite, compare notes, and potentially pursue a class-action approach.

## CHAPTER 22
## WHAT ARE THE KIDS SAYING?

One afternoon, as I found myself at a local coffee shop, my attention was captured by a group of young individuals who, judging by their demeanor and energy, seemed to be high school-aged. Ever the avid "people watcher," I couldn't resist observing them. They exuded a contagious enthusiasm, their laughter echoing through the air. Unable to resist my curiosity, I leaned in and decided to strike up a conversation. Being high school-age kids, I am sure they loved it.

"Excuse me, hi, how old are ya?" I inquired. Their ages varied, but they were all in high school. Surprisingly, they welcomed my interruption and were eager to engage in conversation. As we chatted, I discovered a unique aspect about them—they were all homeschooled. While some had experienced public schooling during their earlier years, others had navigated through both middle and high school in the homeschooling realm.

My curiosity led me to inquire about neurodivergences, a term encompassing conditions like anxiety, ADHD/ADD, and Autism. To my surprise, every hand shot up around the table. A shared recognition dawned upon them; they were not alone in their experiences. I allowed them a moment to absorb the realization before delving into their thoughts on traditional schooling.

Their responses, a chorus of disdain for conventional education, painted a vivid picture. One girl blurted out, "hated it," while a young man shared that the traditional teaching methods didn't resonate with him. Despite struggling in a traditional school environment, he proudly announced that he had earned his associate degree before turning 18. Alternative methods had been the key to unlocking his potential and sustaining his love for learning.

Others echoed sentiments of disliking teachers, citing instances of unkindness and public humiliation. Some expressed boredom, while others simply couldn't articulate why they detested traditional schooling. It became apparent that the one-size-fits-all approach didn't suit their diverse learning styles.

In the midst of our conversation, I couldn't help but commend them on their resilience. "Even on your worst day, you are unstoppable," I remarked. With gratitude and understanding, I allowed them to return to their day, acknowledging that the last thing they needed was an older observer disrupting their camaraderie.

Reflecting on the conversation, I pondered the prospect of homeschooling for my own son. The stories I heard resonated deeply, and I questioned whether my child could thrive in a different educational setting. Recollections of the challenges brought about by the COVID-19 pandemic surfaced, but this seemed like an entirely different avenue.

Recalling a message from a former student during the turmoil surrounding our school, I realized the widespread impact of these issues. The young man, a fellow alum from our Charter School, shared his similar experiences and the involvement of the OCR in his case. His validation of my concerns provided both solace and a stark realization of the systemic issues at hand.

As I continued observing the group of homeschooled teenagers, I found myself contemplating the necessary steps to address the larger issue. How many more students were silently struggling within the confines of traditional education? The question lingered, urging me to consider what actions could be taken to alleviate the challenges faced by these students and, undoubtedly, countless others.

## CHAPTER 23
# MEDIA

Mark Zuckerberg's statement, "Social media is not just a platform, it's a reflection of society," is intriguing, isn't it? However, upon deeper reflection, one might argue that social media doesn't always present an accurate portrayal of society. It often seems to project a distorted or filtered version of reality. While social media may be a portrayal of society, remember that information put on there is being controlled through filtering, so does begs the question: does social media always show you what is happening around you, or does it only show you what you want to see? The question arises: in a world where truth can seem elusive, can we truly believe everything we encounter, especially on these platforms? There's a lingering concern that what we read or see might not necessarily be genuine, making one wonder about the value of the information consumed. The hope remains that the time invested in absorbing content, like this book, isn't in vain, but rather sparks critical thinking and exploration of its themes and messages.

The media landscape has historically been influenced by biases. In the past, it largely reflected what governments wanted the public to perceive, restricting access to selective information. Even the partisan press, characteristic of specific eras in journalism, tended to offer a singular perspective, omitting alternative viewpoints.

Today, judgment seems to thrive, albeit under the guise of reviews. There's an undeniable fascination with reviews—receiving them, leaving them, and acknowledging their potential to shape perceptions. The power of a review, or a cascade of them, has the ability to make or break individuals, businesses, or entities. Notably, platforms like Google and Facebook have emerged as the epicenters of these reviews. A company's longevity is often correlated with the accumulation of reviews, an indication of its track record over time. Digital marketing experts emphasize the significance of maintaining a positive array of Google reviews for businesses.

Yet, amidst this emphasis on reviews, it's essential to recognize a practice where companies engage in "scrubbing" Google reviews. This involves the strategic removal of negative feedback and the curation of reviews to present a more favorable image. This manipulation raises questions about the authenticity and reliability of the feedback available online.

In essence, the evolving landscape of media, from historical biases to the current dominance of reviews on digital platforms, invites a critical assessment of the authenticity and manipulation prevalent within the information we encounter.

As things began to take a turn for the worse, an instinctual feeling of not being alone nudged me into action, prompting me to seek solidarity with others who might share similar experiences. Initially, I turned to Google, anticipating a wealth of information, yet there were only three reviews available. This scarcity struck me as odd, and my professional background in marketing alerted me to the potential tactics organizations employ to shield themselves from negative exposure. Considering this Charter school's extensive existence spanning over two decades, it seemed implausible that only three reviews existed.

Driven by an inherent curiosity and a commitment to uncover the truth, I delved deeper into my investigation. My search extended beyond the confines of the school's immediate Google profile. I scoured various sources, discovering a plethora of platforms hosting reviews for schools across the country. It was a breakthrough moment when I finally located the unfiltered perspectives I sought. In these overlooked corners, I encountered numerous reviews that resonated with the culture and experiences I had encountered firsthand.

What struck me profoundly was the influx of reviews authored by students themselves—individuals who had grown up within the very walls of the Charter school that my journey revolved around. Their voices painted a vivid picture of the institution's ethos and practices, offering a firsthand account of its impact.

In my quest for comprehensive information, I stumbled upon valuable resources like Greatschools.org and Niche.com. These platforms not only provided reviews but also presented valuable demographic insights about the schools, enriching my understanding of the broader context surrounding educational institutions like the Charter school in question.

The moment arrived when I felt compelled to challenge the reality I found myself in, testing the validity of my observations. In an attempt to contribute my own perspective, I posted a review on Google, only to witness its disappearance within a span of fewer than thirty days. This turn of events prompted a cascade of questions and uncertainties.

The vanishing act of my review led to a perplexing realization. While unconfirmed by the school, this incident opened up a realm of possibilities that demanded contemplation. Would an educational institution, supposedly dedicated to fostering learning and growth, invest resources in erasing or suppressing genuine feedback?

This newfound revelation sparked a whirlwind of thoughts. It beckoned me to ponder the underlying motives: Why the inclination to expunge or conceal opinions, whether positive or negative? Shouldn't an institution, especially one entrusted with education, embrace transparency and the diversity of viewpoints to evolve and improve?

The deliberate effort to control the narrative by silencing dissenting voices raises red flags. It not only questions the integrity and authenticity of the institution but also casts doubts on the motivations behind such actions. Is it a quest to project an idealized image, hiding flaws that could potentially be addressed and rectified? Or is there a deeper, systemic issue that the school is reluctant to address?

This unfolding scenario challenges conventional perceptions about the role of educational institutions in society. It prompts a critical examination of the power dynamics at play, urging us to question why any entity, especially one responsible for shaping young minds, would opt to curate or manipulate the reality of their narrative.

In my urgent attempt to expose the unfolding wrongdoings, I reached out to every local media outlet in the Charlotte Metro area and even expanded my efforts to larger publications like The Times, Washington Post, and Huffington Post. Unfortunately, the responses from the larger publications often redirected me to seek help for suicide, rather than addressing the pressing concerns I was raising. There was a glimmer of hope when I thought I had connected with a local reporter from WCNC. We met over coffee, and I earnestly shared every detail and piece of evidence I had gathered regarding the situation. However, her engagement was fleeting, and soon after our meeting, I found myself ignored—ghosted without explanation.

Understanding that reporters grapple with numerous stories daily, and in a world where sensational news grabs immediate attention, I couldn't help but feel that an issue as significant as this warranted, at the very least, a meaningful conversation. My intentions were anchored in the pursuit of truth and justice, supported by a plethora of evidence. Factual journalism holds great importance for me, as my purpose was not to disparage the school but rather to sound an alarm and seek assistance. Yet, this uphill battle felt relentless, testing my resolve at every turn.

A friend of mine, a talented photographer with a journalism degree, suggested reaching out to another reporter, one she knew personally. Nervousness consumed me as I sat across from this journalist at the Neighborhood Café in Huntersville. I wrestled with wanting to convey every detail without overwhelming the reporter, fearing that any misstep might scare off my last hope for recourse. As we sipped iced teas, the journalist pulled out a recorder, initiating a conversation. Handing over piles of printed communications and a timeline of events, I recounted the ordeal. Despite the difficulty of the subject matter, an unsettling feeling of embarrassment lingered throughout the discussion.

At times, doubts crept in. Had my unwavering pursuit of justice led me down a path where I was now perceived as irrational or excessively fixated on the issue? The worry of being dismissed as the 'crazy lady' plagued my thoughts. However, until this encounter, no one had taken the time to genuinely sit down and listen to my story.

Amidst the weight of my consuming concerns, a persistent but smaller thought lingered—a niggling worry about the behavior of the victims. It's distressing to acknowledge that many victims are subjected to gaslighting, an insidious tactic that places blame on them for the injustices they endure.

This particular thought, while not dominating my mind, felt deeply unsettling. The idea that victims might be manipulated into believing they're at fault for the circumstances they face is abhorrent. It's a concept that, even though it didn't occupy the forefront of my thoughts, remains a disquieting aspect within the larger context of the situation.

Recognizing the existence of this thought and vehemently rejecting it underscores a strong stance against the manipulation and mistreatment of victims. It serves as a testament to a deeper understanding of the psychological dynamics at play, where victims are unfairly made to question their own experiences and responsibilities.

Amidst the greater challenges at hand, this smaller thought signifies a troubling aspect of societal dynamics. It challenges our fundamental beliefs in justice and fairness, sparking a determined resolve to counter such insinuations and stand in solidarity with those who have been wronged.

The release of the article was a watershed moment for me, and I will forever be indebted to the courageous journalist behind it. He took a bold step, crafting and publishing an article that sent reverberations through our pretentious town. His impeccable professionalism is a tribute to genuine journalism everywhere, and it shook the very foundations of the community.

Following the article's publication, there was an influx of people reaching out to me. Parents started sharing their own stories and insights into the wrongdoings perpetrated by the school. However, as time passed, I found myself increasingly perplexed by the lack of response from the wider media, despite the attention the article garnered.

It was during one of my routine errand runs that an unexpected Facebook request brought a surprising revelation. A woman shared something pivotal with me—a podcast featuring the superintendent. They were positioned as the "guest" and purported "expert" in crisis management. In this podcast, they outlined a strategy to mitigate negative exposure during a crisis, directing their message to district administrators willing to listen.

This discovery provided the elusive answer to the lingering question that had haunted me for months. It unveiled a deliberate roadmap meticulously crafted by the superintendent, shedding light on their calculated approach to handling and reducing negative attention amidst the crisis the school faced, despite any wrongdoing on their part.

Sitting alone in my car, I listened intently to the entire podcast. A storm brewed within me; anger churned in my stomach. The level of self-aggrandizement exhibited by this individual was nothing short of surreal. However, the "ah ha" moment hit when I discovered that the school allocated a substantial budget for "media relationships." Why would a school invest in creating favorability with the media?

As the podcast unfolded, they openly discussed their meticulously crafted strategy for managing media responses and eradicating any hint of negative exposure. It was a jarring revelation that they were essentially buying favor from local reporters. It wasn't that I was entirely shocked they'd stoop so low, but rather the disbelief that a significant number of journalists were willing participants in this charade.

In that solitary moment in the car, confusion and helplessness enveloped me. It felt like everything I had painstakingly planned was unraveling before my eyes. Lost in a sea of conflicting emotions, I, too, was on the verge of completing a degree in communications and had explored journalism enough to understand its ethical underpinnings. Yet, this revelation left me feeling betrayed, creating an overwhelming sense of distrust towards nearly everyone around me.

The WCNC reporter indirectly confirmed this unsettling truth, albeit in more subtle terms. She conveyed how reporters often tend to favor schools, hoping for exclusive stories linked to larger events. It was an eye-opener, realizing that organizations commonly "take care of" journalists for their own ulterior motives.

Months later, amidst a moment of profound desperation and clarity, I resolved to share my story in its entirety—a synthesis of personal experience intertwined with the knowledge I had gathered. The WCNC reporter had initially intended to turn this into a comprehensive special, even arranging for an in-studio panel. That's why it struck me as profoundly odd when all communication abruptly ceased.

Questions flooded my mind—had she been silenced by someone else, possibly through manipulation or inducements? Was she coerced into halting the investigation by forces who were perhaps "taken care of" by the same entities being exposed? The abrupt halt in communication left me grappling with a range of unsettling possibilities, casting doubt on the integrity of the process and the motivations behind the sudden silence.

We may never fully comprehend the situation, but what remains clear is that an unimaginable event was unfolding. The media seemed intertwined with the school, deliberately censoring reviews, and obstructing avenues for the truth on public platforms. In this scenario, mothers like me were the villains.

# CHAPTER 24
## FIOA

The Freedom of Information Act (FOIA) is a vital federal law that empowers individuals to access information held by the federal government. It essentially serves as a vehicle for transparency, enabling citizens to request specific documents, records, or data from federal entities. The process allows for the retrieval of various types of information, contributing to accountability and an informed citizenry.

On the state level, analogous to FOIA, many states have their own versions of public information requests. For instance, in North Carolina, this is regulated under section 132.1 of the General Assembly statutes. While its functions are similar to the federal FOIA, it is often colloquially referred to as the "state FIOA request." This state-level legislation outlines the procedures and rights associated with requesting public information and specifies whom to approach within the state government to make such requests.

However, it's essential to note that while these laws mandate the provision of information, there are instances where charges may apply, typically for duplication costs. Nonetheless, individuals have the right to contest these charges and request waivers under certain circumstances. If you are requesting documents from a school, there should not be a cost associated with the request, especially being that they are delivered digitally.

Regarding educational requests, there's a specified timeframe of 20 days within which schools are required to respond to such inquiries. However, when it comes to delivering the requested information, the state allows a more flexible timeline, generally referring to it as being within a "reasonable" period. Unfortunately, these state requests are often deemed "toothless" due to the absence of strict consequences for schools failing to deliver the requested documents within the specified timelines.

To provide context, a public information request offers an opportunity to access any information stored on the school's servers pertaining to either yourself or your child. It's important to recognize that even if the school does not explicitly present itself as a public school or a public charter, it still falls under the purview of public information requests due to its classification.

When making these requests, it's crucial to ensure they are submitted in writing. Additionally, any sensitive or irrelevant information, such as details regarding other students or confidential organizational data that doesn't pertain to the request, may be redacted by the school's attorney.

Overall, navigating the process of requesting public information involves understanding both federal and state laws, abiding by specified procedures, and exercising your rights to access information while being mindful of confidentiality and other legal considerations.

These requests are to be sent to a school official, within a public charter school it will most commonly be the superintendent, I would also personally CC the board. I have had experiences at our charter school where the board played a lovely game of hiding the ball. If you send it to everyone, then the opportunity for the person responsible to pretend they never received it is a lot less. Also, make sure you reference the state records request not the FOIA.

*North Carolina Sample FOIA Request/State Public Records Request template*

*[Your Name]*

*[Street Address]*

*[City, ST ZIP Code]*

*[Date]*

*[Name of Custodian of Records]*

*[Title]*

*[Company Name]*

*[Street Address]*

*[City, ST ZIP Code]*

*Dear [custodian of records]*

*Under the North Carolina Public Records Law, G.S. §132-1., I am requesting an opportunity to inspect or obtain copies of public records that [Describe the records or information sought with enough detail for the public agency to respond. Be as specific as your knowledge of the available records will allow. But it is more important to describe the information you are seeking.]*

*If there are any fees for searching or copying these records, please inform me if the cost will exceed $_____. However, I would also like to request a waiver of all fees in that the disclosure of the requested information is in the public interest and will contribute significantly to the public's understanding of _____ [Here, you can identify yourself as a representative of the news media if applicable and state that your request is related to news gathering purposes.] This information is not being sought for commercial purposes.*

*The law requires that you respond to and fulfill this request "as promptly as possible." If you expect a significant delay in responding to and fulfilling this request, please contact me with information about when I might expect copies or the ability to inspect the requested records.*

*If you deny any or all of this request, please cite each specific exemption you feel justifies the refusal to release the information and notify me of the appeal procedures available to me under the law.*

*Thank you for considering my request.*

*Sincerely,*

*[Your Name]*

*[Your Phone number]*

Throughout this entire ordeal—a rollercoaster ride from hell—I've consistently felt an overwhelming sense of the unknown. Not just about statutes, laws, or the procedures for filing complaints, but a deeper sense that the school might be culpable for more than I've even come to realize.

During this tumultuous journey, I connected with another mother navigating her own challenges within the school system. As fate would have it, our paths crossed on the road to addressing our respective issues, and our connection evolved beyond friendship; we became allies. She suggested filing an FIOA request and explained its essence. This prompted numerous questions, leading me back to the realms of Google once again.

Seeking guidance, I reached out to our attorney to understand what the request might uncover and if any potential hurdles were on the horizon. Drafting an email akin to the template I'd prepared earlier; I sent it off to both the board and the superintendent. Miraculously, within a mere 48 hours, a response arrived, acknowledging receipt of my request. Now, all that remained was to wait.

...and wait.

Today marks 150 days since I submitted the request to the school. It wasn't surprising that the school didn't fully comply with the request; it seems they believe themselves to be above the rules. Apparently, a child's suicidal ideations are just a "perception" to them—and a mistaken one at that.

Coincidentally, I happen to know a North Carolina State Senator. During one of our casual conversations, I mentioned the recent events within the school system. He suggested submitting a Freedom of Information Act (FOIA) request. I chuckled, informing him that I had already done so, but it was abundantly clear that the school had no intention of complying.

To clarify, I did receive a small batch of documents from the school about 48 days after the initial request. Their attorney sent a link, mentioning that due to the volume of documents, they would be sent in stages. However, that was the last communication from the attorney, despite our persistent attempts to follow up.

While going through every document the school's attorney sent, I discovered images taken from my social media accounts within the last 3 months. The fact that these were circulating through the school's servers led me to believe they were conducting some form of research. Surprisingly, I found this empowering—their concern about me was evident in their efforts to dig into my personal life. Most of the documents comprised Schoology posts with my comments.

Referring back to that "draft" document I mentioned earlier—its existence triggered a recollection of an email from the school counselor. The initial communication informed me that my son had been banging his head against the dry-erase board due to being "disappointed" in his mock EOG grade. However, the version obtained through the FIOA request revealed an alarming omission: the word "depression."

Upon further investigation, it became evident that the superintendent had altered the counselor's email, and the school's licensed psychologist had sanctioned the revision before sending us an edited version. That alone should call into question their license. This discovery through the FIOA request exposed the school's deceit and attempts to cover up signs of severe mental health issues. This revelation fueled my determination to push even harder. I was certain this irrefutable evidence showcased their negligence, potentially reaching the level of criminality had my son taken his own life.

Subsequent to this revelation, there was complete silence from the school and their attorney. I took part in conversations with various elected officials in Raleigh, which proved immensely enlightening. Through these discussions, I was connected with North Carolina's Director for the Board of Charters. Following her guidance, I reached out, briefing her on the situation and expressing my need for assistance, as she had alluded to during our conversation.

The Director promptly took action; upon receiving the attachments of all communications, including the initial request, she engaged her office to contact the school. Their response claimed the attorney was deeply occupied and diligently working on the request, citing supposed prior contact with me.

In hopes that this would spur them into action, I waited patiently for a few weeks. However, as time passed without any communication from either the attorney or the school, I decided to reach out to the Director once more. In my email, I clarified that contrary to what was conveyed, I hadn't been in contact with the attorney since the transmission of the first "batch" of documents. Furthermore, I highlighted the possibility of incriminating documents that could expose the school to negative repercussions. Although I couldn't ascertain the precise reason for their silence, it seemed a plausible explanation.

Evidently, the Director had been provided with a version of events that deviated from the truth. We mutually agreed to reconvene after the holidays.

The existence of the Public Information Act begs the question: if there are no real consequences for not adhering to it, what purpose does it serve? Schools seem to understand that there's little to no punishment for non-compliance, leading them to simply stop responding—unless someone of significance takes notice of our pleas for assistance, which is so incredibly wrong.

During one of my meetings with the OCR attorney, as we were preparing for scheduled mediation, I expressed my concern about proceeding without having all the necessary information. I followed every prescribed step in the correct order. It seemed futile to engage in mediation without the complete facts. The OCR attorney's response struck me like a bullet to the chest. Their question about the usefulness of having this information and what I hoped to gain from it left me astounded. It felt as if ethical considerations in legislation were nonexistent.

Unveiling something substantial, I realized the school would never admit to it. How could I be expected to enter a room aimed at repairing and implementing systemic changes for the greater good if the school lacked genuine intentions to rectify the situation?

It's akin to being caught in a lie, knowing there's still more they're hiding—it's unsettling, to say the least. Holding the school accountable for even one aspect became crucial to me. However, up to this point, It hadn't dawned on me to document this journey in an actual book. Uncertain about what to do with the gathered information, the media remained indifferent, likely due to the school's efforts in "building relationships" with them. Meanwhile, the OCR's questioning of the purpose of transparency only added to the sense of hopelessness.

It's disheartening to realize that when it comes to advocating for our children, we seem to be on our own. It evokes a sense of nostalgia for the days of the civil rights movement when those who drove change were bold, brave, and unwavering in their persistence. Nowadays, leaders often seem to be veiled in dishonesty, and this realization is truly horrifying.

Given the previous outcome, I harbored little hope that the Director's efforts would yield any tangible results, as our previous interactions hadn't led to any substantial changes. She mentioned the likelihood of getting in touch after the holidays. So, you can imagine my surprise when, just a few days after reaching out to her, I received an email from the school's attorney over the weekend.

*Barring something unforeseen, I will complete my review and produce to you any additional responsive documents on or before Friday, December 15th. Just to recap, there were more than 10,000 items to review, and we've produced a significant number of documents for you already.*

*I apologize for my delay.*

Exercising every bit of my self-restraint, I refrained from firing back a snide response. It was tempting to point out the obvious: around 30 duplicated documents among the bunch that he sent. Recognizing the situation, I chose the higher path. After all, the last thing a charter school desires is the Board of Charters prying into their operations, especially if there are questionable activities taking place.

As the promised date of December 15th slipped away without any response or delivery of documents from the attorney, frustration and disappointment mounted. It was baffling—no unforeseen circumstances had been communicated, yet it seemed inevitable that excuses might sprout forth when facing the Director of NC OCS (Office of Charter Schools).

The desire to be a proverbial "fly on the wall" in that room surged. Do they operate in a closed circle, familiar with one another's ways? Do they perhaps jest at our expense, making light of our earnest concerns? Questions about the integrity of those involved echoed loudly. Is there a shred of ethics or compassion left among them? The attorney's lack of honesty was glaring, and his skillful weaving of lies to shield a school was disheartening. This realization cut deep and instilled an indescribable fear that this might be the end of the road.

Every avenue has been meticulously explored, every option exhausted. However, the stark reality persists: if the schools aren't willing, they won't comply. The pressing need for more individuals willing to challenge the status quo emerged—individuals ready to confront and reshape what is considered acceptable.

Reaching out to the Director again was an act of diminishing hope, though this did not mean that I was not going to let her know that he yet again failed to deliver. Expectations were tempered, but the urgency to share accumulated knowledge couldn't be delayed any further. The tactic seemed clear: to sow doubt among parents, to erode our trust in our instincts. It begged the question: if the NC Office of Charter Schools can't enforce adherence, could it be that our charter schools possess excessive autonomy?

The longing for change mingled with frustration, creating an unsettling atmosphere. It hinted at the possibility that the very freedom granted to these institutions might be wielded in ways detrimental to the greater good.

# CHAPTER 25
# TRUITT'S PARENTS ADVISORY COMMISSION

On February 23, 2022, Catherine Truitt, the State Superintendent of North Carolina, made an impactful announcement: the establishment of a parent advisory commission aimed at fostering a stronger connection between the educational system and parents. The Parent Advisory Commission, a pioneering step in North Carolina's commitment to collaboration, seeks to harness the collective wisdom and insights of parents. This groundbreaking initiative aimed to assemble a robust panel comprising 48 K-12 parents hailing from diverse regions across the state of North Carolina.

The fundamental goal of this commission was to amplify the voices of parents within the realm of student education. It was envisioned as a vital platform to bridge the gap between educational policies and the real-life experiences of families. The overwhelming response from the community reflected the eagerness of over 3,000 parents vying for a spot within this influential commission, illustrating the deep-rooted interest and commitment to shaping the educational landscape.

An essential feature of this commission was its deliberate inclusivity. Membership extended to parents with children enrolled in various educational settings, ranging from traditional public schools to charter schools, homeschooling, and private institutions. This inclusive approach ensured a broad spectrum of representation across different educational choices, emphasizing the need for diverse perspectives and feedback.

The role of this advisory board of parents was to offer guidance, valuable insights, and constructive feedback to educational leaders and policymakers. Their focus encompassed a wide array of educational facets, including curriculum development, student well-being, innovative teaching methodologies, and policies that impact the educational journey of children.

By bringing together parents from different educational backgrounds, the commission aimed to foster meaningful discussions, promote collaboration, and create a platform where diverse voices could contribute to the enhancement of educational policies and practices. Ultimately, this initiative sought to build a more inclusive, responsive, and effective educational system that caters to the needs and aspirations of every child in North Carolina.

The unveiling of this commission was not widely publicized, and truth be told, I was one of those individuals who hadn't delved into the intricate world of educational politics until recently. Often, many parents find themselves not closely engaged in the educational system until faced with a situation that demands their attention. It's a common sentiment – we tend to navigate through our daily lives, and it's only when something goes awry that we feel compelled to dive deeper into understanding the underlying issues.

I've encountered advice in the past suggesting that if I disagreed with the system, the best recourse was to exercise my voting rights. Until there was a pressing reason to immerse myself in the labyrinth of educational politics, I lacked the inclination to do so. If we are being honest, I am questioning the idea that participation yields results. I find it hard to believe that voters would neglect and vote against programs that are designed to aid in the protection of equal education opportunities.

Regarding the commission's composition, it's intriguing to note the deliberate inclusion of representatives from different educational domains, including traditional public schools, charter schools, homeschooling, and private institutions. The allocation of specific slots from prominent counties in each region further emphasizes the aim for diverse representation and insights.

However, despite the noble intentions and the promise of transparency through recorded minutes, there seems to be an air of disappointment surrounding the content of these documents. They appear to lack substantial discussions or meaningful contributions, raising questions about the effectiveness of these sessions. Moreover, the absence of Superintendent Truitt from these meetings, as noted by her non-involvement in initiating proceedings or contributing feedback, raises concerns about the leadership's engagement in this initiative.

Superintendent Truitt's emphasis on the pivotal role of parents in fostering academic excellence and the positive impact of parental involvement on students' attitudes toward learning echoes a widely accepted sentiment. Her ambition to encourage families to participate in district-level decisions is commendable, and the establishment of this commission appears to be a step in that direction. However, its practical implementation and the tangible impact it creates seem to be falling short of initial expectations.

In essence, while the intention behind the commission is admirable and aligned with the goal of engaging parents in educational policies, its current execution and outcomes suggest a need for recalibration and more substantive involvement from all stakeholders, including the educational leadership, to ensure its effectiveness in effecting positive change within the educational landscape.

I'm keen on considering the data referenced by Truitt regarding student success outcomes. It's essential to question what the data reveals when the impediment to a child's education stems from the school itself. Moreover, it's crucial to refrain from shaming parents for their work commitments, as it's rarely the case that they don't want to be involved in their child's education. Simply put, it is unfair and pretentious to assume a parent's involvement as a measure to determine a child's success, not when the system is as broken as it is.

Navigating the education system alongside a child with special needs is an immense challenge. At times, it feels nearly impossible. While certain ideas proposed by educational authorities might seem promising and gain support, they often create an illusion, leading ultimately to dead ends.

It's vital that every parent who has experienced the struggle of advocating for a child with special needs within the education system knows that the difficulty is acknowledged. Instead of merely endorsing initiatives for the sake of popularity, we need solutions that break through the barriers and genuinely support these children and their families.

## CHAPTER 26
# WHAT DOES CHANGE LOOK LIKE...

I was once advised that simply complaining without offering a solution isn't productive. While I acknowledge that constantly criticizing without positivity can affect mental health, this advice is often directed at those labeled as 'complainers.' I admit, I tend to voice concerns about areas that could be improved. Although I may not always have all the answers, I take pride in contributing thoughts and conducting research to find potential solutions.

When vehicles consistently speed down a neighborhood street, it often leads residents to unite and petition the city for the installation of speed bumps. This typically involves a straightforward process and could potentially save a child's life while they're playing. This is a great example of implementing a change. It seems odd that people are so fast to throw a stop sign up to save a child's life, but not hold a school accountable for their actions. Actions that could potentially cost a child their life.

However, within our education system, navigating the process often feels like encountering dead ends and unexpected U-turns. Accessing information or solutions frequently hinges on personal connections rather than following a transparent and accessible procedure. The state seems proficient at concealing crucial information and procedures, which creates barriers preventing individuals from easily understanding or accessing the necessary channels for resolution. There's a deliberate effort to maintain opacity, discouraging outspoken individuals from entering and challenging the status quo.

While technically a process exists, it's labyrinthine and filled with complexities, making it an uphill battle. Take, for instance, the option to address grievances through the Administrative Procedures Act, particularly under § 150B-20, allowing petitioning an agency to adopt a rule. However, deciphering this legal document is akin to navigating a cryptic manuscript. The dense language and legal jargon within this Act make it immensely challenging for the average person to comprehend, let alone navigate effectively. Not to mention the intricacies involved in the Administrative Procedures Act, which often create barriers for individuals attempting to seek resolutions through § 150B-20. For the record when it comes to understanding this I am below average, my head spins and I immediately become discouraged.

It becomes evident that the state's grievance process urgently needs enhancements to be more accessible and comprehensible for the public. The current convoluted nature of the system discourages individuals from seeking legitimate changes and improvements. Simplifying the language, providing clear guidelines, and establishing transparent pathways for grievance resolution would empower individuals to voice their concerns without feeling overwhelmed by bureaucratic procedures.

The need for a more user-friendly and equitable process is evident. Citizens shouldn't be deterred from advocating for necessary reforms due to the inherent complexities within the system. A reformed grievance process would not only encourage greater participation but also ensure that the concerns of individuals within the education system are addressed fairly and promptly, creating a more conducive environment for positive change and progress.

It's important to recognize the difference between a rule and a procedure within the system. If a rule is in place, proposing a change involves either creating a new rule or suggesting an amendment to an existing one. However, when dealing with a procedure that lacks formal codification as a rule, the challenge becomes more intricate. In such cases, the proposal of a rule becomes necessary to counterbalance the existing procedure.

The actual submission process for proposing these changes often lacks clarity and can be vague, if outlined at all. There are stipulations tied to the fiscal year and the publication of these rules and amendments. However, a definitive and concise guide on who can initiate these changes and the specific steps involved in the submission process is notably absent. This lack of clarity adds another layer of complexity and ambiguity to an already intricate system.

With all these complexities, it's apparent that there's an urgent need for substantial improvements. Despite the existence of a process, the convoluted nature and lack of transparency present formidable obstacles. However, it's essential to acknowledge that a process does indeed exist, and there's a strong determination to navigate through its intricacies and understand it thoroughly.

While it's evident that there's a lot of work ahead, the commitment remains unwavering. Despite the complexities and ambiguities, there's an intention to delve into the system's intricacies and uncover the pathways to initiate necessary changes. This determination to understand and navigate the system serves as a testament to resilience and dedication toward effecting meaningful improvements, and I will continue to make sense.

Throughout my experience, the overall lack of investigation that takes place could use some work. I don't think expecting the investigators to actually investigate is asking too much. I would like to see the DPI adopt a similar to that of the OCR. If the DPI would take the time to speak with the parents who are filing the complaints, walking through the complaint would yield several benefits.

Rather than superficially reviewing a complaint and swiftly moving on, there's an invaluable opportunity to genuinely comprehend the underlying intentions behind it. Establishing a channel for communication could significantly reduce the influx of repetitive, irrelevant, and unnecessary complaints, ultimately lightening the burden on the Department of Public Instruction (DPI). However, this approach might also mean an increase in claims against schools, which the state seems to be hesitant about currently.

There's a pressing need for a formal appeals process within the DPI framework. Such a process would allow parents or individuals to submit supporting evidence subsequent to the completion of document requests, enabling them to scrutinize the school's defense against the claim. This setup would compel schools to provide accurate and truthful statements, fostering transparency and accountability in addressing complaints.

Moreover, instituting a formal appeal request mechanism is essential. This step would provide a structured avenue for individuals to contest decisions they perceive as unjust or inaccurate. As it stands now, there is no real accountability had on the DPI, their actions are going unnoticed and are in desperate need of evaluation.

Within the current DPI process, it's imperative to introduce a review system for all filed complaints. This step would involve having a fresh set of eyes examine the final decisions, ensuring a fair and impartial evaluation. It's been highlighted that had a different individual reviewed a particular case, they might have interpreted it differently and possibly favored the child over the school.

This underscores the necessity of implementing a comprehensive review process that allows for diverse perspectives to weigh in on decisions. It's essential to create a system that not only upholds the interests of schools but also prioritizes the welfare and rights of students. By introducing checks and balances into the DPI's complaint resolution mechanism, it becomes possible to cultivate a fair and just environment for addressing grievances within the education system.

Beyond the formal amendments required, a fundamental shift in mindset is crucial to drive any substantial change forward. It's not just an expectation; it should be the norm ingrained in society, an unwavering principle that we uphold. As parents, it's incumbent upon us not only to comprehend the current state of affairs but also to staunchly advocate for the way things ought to be. This steadfast determination to rectify the unethical treatment of our children necessitates transforming these ideas into resolute demands, voiced with amplified intensity.

While some might label this persistence as an annoyance, I perceive it as unwavering determination. What certain authorities might deem as accosting; I view as directness in seeking justice. It's imperative to be assertive and unyielding because what's at stake here is irreplaceable – the well-being and future of our children.

Engaging with directors and elected officials who confidently stand at podiums promising the world upon receiving our votes is crucial. We must hold them accountable by posing tough questions and demanding substantive answers. Accepting defeat in the face of injustice or negligence is not an option.

Sending emails, making calls, and participating in open dialogues are just some of the means through which we can assert our demands for change. Persistence in seeking resolutions to issues affecting our children's welfare is not merely an option; it's an obligation. Our collective insistence on fairness and integrity should resonate louder than ever before.

It's vital to continuously challenge the status quo, fostering an environment where the rights and dignity of our children are safeguarded without compromise. Never underestimate the power of persistence and unwavering advocacy, for therein lies the potential to effect real, meaningful change.

# CONCLUSION

Throughout my journey as a mother, an underlying feeling persisted, a sensation that something was off. For many years I operated within the boundaries of a neurotypical mentality. It wasn't until the one person I loved more than life itself, opened my eyes to an entirely different world veiled behind an unfamiliar door. Behind that door, clarity prevailed, prompting me to question why this revelation wasn't the common norm. The key to unlocking this door lay in the simplicity of perceiving it.

My child, an unparalleled source of inspiration, has unraveled within me the finest version of myself I've ever encountered, this child of mine inspires me to be the best version of myself I have ever known. Every action, every effort I exert, is solely directed towards providing him with the universe, even aspects I have yet to uncover. Everything I do I do for him. I often find myself assuming the role of his filter, gathering and safeguarding all that surrounds him, careful not to let in any harm.

The puzzle pieces started aligning only when I began to delve deeper into what I had merely categorized as cute or quirky. For numerous years, it was solely about him, and never did I attempt to attach reasoning to his behaviors. As a toddler, most captured moments showcased little blurs around his hands—he'd exhibit excitement through flapping, a gesture whose significance was indicative of autism I only learned about a year ago. When we introduced him to kayaking, it was interesting. His delight was palpable as he leaned over the boat's edge for two hours, entranced by the sensation of water streaming through his fingers. A nightly ritual sees him standing in the shower for 45 minutes, finding solace in the comforting embrace of cascading water. It all comes together, and it's exciting to watch him observe him take in the world differently. It is when we see things in a different way that new observations and discoveries are made.

My time is dedicated to understanding the nuances that bring him joy. This pursuit of knowledge and comprehension comes at no tangible cost; it's simply a commitment to study and learn. Kayaking, for instance, was an adventure, but I couldn't fathom the depth of experience he would derive from it. To this day, he still tells me how satisfying the water in his fingers was. This, I've come to realize, is life in its truest essence—about learning and growing, embracing every moment as a conduit for growth.

Yet, this fundamental aspect of exploration and joy in learning was systematically robbed from him by the confines of traditional schooling. Instead of nurturing his unique passions, they burdened him with the weight of feeling inadequate for simply being himself, to the extent that he contemplated the value of his existence. This became his narrative, our narrative, one that has presented me with an opportunity to extend a helping hand to others navigating similar paths.

Not having a rule book isn't the worst thing in the world; in fact, it's liberating. It grants you the freedom to craft your own guidelines and to design a unique path that suits both you and your children. Especially when parenting a child with special needs, the conventional rulebook becomes irrelevant; what matters most is finding what genuinely works for your family.

As I gather my thoughts to conclude, I realize the importance of passing on my story so that you, too, can embark on your journey, crafting your narrative. Amidst this rush, a lingering sensation nudges me, urging me to ensure you're equipped with every ounce of insight I've gathered. I aspire to fill your heart with the confidence I might have lacked initially, encouraging you to fiercely pursue your battle. I have found myself worrying if I have given you not enough, however, it's more than I had and I know I am not alone.

Fear has been an uninvited companion throughout this experience. It's perplexing how fear and education seem intertwined, often shadowing the clarity we seek. My son, confronted with his own limitations, voiced his struggles, a defining moment that propelled me to gear up and confront challenges head-on.

In such times, it's pivotal not to succumb to fear's grip. Witnessing my son's determination became a rallying cry— an inspiration for me to lace up my boots and charge bravely into the fray.

Reflecting on this journey, I've realized that we're not alone in this struggle. It's a collective endeavor. The idea of 'they can't catch us all' resonates profoundly—we outnumber the challenges, standing united, each voice demanding a more equitable and empathetic system.

Stand tall, one by one, and demand better. Embrace the power of unity, for it is through collective determination that we pave the way for a brighter, more inclusive future for our children and ourselves.

With the fear of retaliation lingering heavy in your mind, be the change you seek, and remember… "The world is a dangerous place, not because of those who do evil, but because of those who look on and do nothing." - Albert Einstein

# EPILOGUE

Progression, in its essence, signifies the continuous process of advancement, development, or forward movement, often unfolding in a systematic or sequential manner. It embodies a journey through various stages or steps leading to a specific outcome or goal, showcasing the concept of advancement over time.

The decision to withdraw the book from publication was motivated by a desire to incorporate the ongoing progression into the narrative. The intention was not to halt at the recounting of a single story; rather, the book served as a catalyst for igniting the flames of change. So, I felt compelled to include recent events. It is the entire purpose of this project.

A pivotal moment occurred when my persistent efforts led to an audience with the Director of Public Instruction, Dr. Carol Ann Hudgens. The invitation to a meeting in Raleigh marked a significant step forward, evoking a profound sense of excitement. The anticipation did not stem from a preconceived notion of meeting a key figure or a certainty of imminent change; instead, it was the prospect of progress.

A three-hour drive to Raleigh allowed time for reflection on proposed solutions that seemed flawless in my mind. The goal was clear – to present ideas that could instigate positive change. The focus, however, was not solely on addressing a personal grievance, as egregious as it was. Rather, it became a platform to trigger a broader desire for process improvement – a genuine commitment to progression.

Arriving ahead of schedule, moments of doubt and self-reflection took hold as I sat in the car. What would this woman think? Was she humoring the situation, or worse, preparing for confrontation? Wrestling with the perception of being cast as a villain a mental reset was imperative. Even the toughest person with the thickest skin still feels hurt. I never wanted to be considered wrong. I never wanted to portray anything other than honest good intentions. The superintendent at the charter school had gotten in and left a lasting impression on me and what I thought about myself. I question myself now more than I ever have. Having had the ability to read the interoffice emails from the staff, I was never someone they tolerated. They would "save" each other from parent teacher meetings, and then laugh about it among themselves. I had read this; I had seen it. While I envy those who can dismiss untrue convictions, I also feel that being conscious of what others get from you is also important. I shook all of this from my mind, and gave myself a quick pep talk, took a deep breath and got out of the car.

The actual encounter defied my expectations. The Director, contrary to imagined scenarios, appeared approachable and kind. Her voice was soft, I was not expecting this, while I had seen her picture this was not what I had created in my mind. The ensuing meeting in the upstairs conference room, joined by her Assistant Director, unfolded in a manner quite different from the anticipated script. Expressing gratitude for the opportunity, a genuine conversation began.

Discussions revolved around a proposed appeals process and the realization that a blanket appeals system might not serve the interests of either parents or the state. The acknowledgment of this fact was met with an openness to explore alternative avenues for improving the process. The exchange of ideas was marked by a mutual understanding of the need for comprehensive solutions.

Initially the idea that even inmates on death row were granted an appeals process; this was what we should do, and no one can argue that, right? She went over the data that the state had collected, and I had no choice but to agree with her, that she was right, which I humorously admitted to not considering on my drive up.

The implementation of an appeals process would be double sided, while allowing parents the right to an appeal it would also allow schools to capitalize on their resources when they are found non-compliant, tying up the DPI with an appeal on most cases. The state would be tied up constantly in appeals and then nothing would be resolved.

I felt very comfortable expressing that this made perfect sense, and that had I considered this, I would have gone back to the drawing board and devised a way for the process to be more thorough and provide families with more support. She was not saying no, because she could. The woman made sense.

Progression.

Delving into the challenges faced by parents, the conversation shifted to a more thorough investigation process and the complexities of completing complaint forms. The realization that a simple review process could have profound implications for the outcome resonated, emphasizing the need for a more supportive approach.

We then walked through the process as it was now and the challenges that parents face when completing the initial forms. She said at times there are cases where the complaint form is clearly not filled out correctly, and the DPI has the right to reach out to those families and confirm their allegations. However, this was not the case for me... and many others. While my forms looked good and the boxes were checked, I had absolutely no idea what I was doing. I was emotional and often exhausted between work and home duties. Had someone called me and reviewed my complaint, let me walk and talk through its contents, would there have been information that could have been applied or submitted to support the case, resulting in a different outcome. Yes.

Dr. Hudgens navigated through the intricacies of potential changes, acknowledging the collaborative effort required. What the supporting organizations in North Carolina would need to know baring any changes, and how those organizations would accept the changes. A lot of things need to happen to change even a sentence in a process such as this. There would need to be many hands on this project in order to make this happen. The prospect of altering established processes underscored the challenges ahead with a timeline discussion pointing towards a potential rollout in July. The DPI uses July as their date, it is when the data collection starts for the year and typically when any amendments are put in place.

Expressing gratitude again, I could not help but to think about the initial perception of the Director as a dismissive figure crumbled, replaced by the realization that open communication and honesty were the keys to progression. I can't say that I regret pestering this woman, but I can say that she was nothing like what I expected.

It's important that I self-reflect on my behaviors and learn from my own course of actions. While I am often painted out to be the villain, I need to remember that I am not, and I need to not let myself take on that role. Passion is a powerful thing and if not used correctly it can become destructive.

While the journey is far from resolving the myriad of problems, this narrative emphasizes the significance of individuals stepping forward and standing up, even in the face of adversity. It serves as a testament to the transformative power of passion, urging individuals to channel it effectively and avoid succumbing to destructive tendencies.

This is a celebration of progress, no matter how incremental, it highlights the importance of honesty in fostering positive change. Those willing to confront challenges, even when the path forward seems daunting. That's progression.

Made in United States
North Haven, CT
09 April 2024